## ABOUT JOOMLA 3 EXPLAINED

You can build great websites with Joomla.

My name is Steve Burge and I'm a Joomla trainer.

During hundreds of Joomla classes in many cities and countries, we've met lots of different types of Joomla learners:

- Joomla learners come from many different backgrounds. They are accountants, florists, photographers, secretaries, factory workers, stay-at-home parents, and people from all walks of life.

- Joomla learners don't need to know anything about websites. Some Joomla learners are professional web designers, but many others have never built a site before and don't know any website code or jargon.

- Joomla learners don't need any experience. We've trained people who went to work the previous week and found their boss saying, "Surprise! You're running our Joomla site!" They often still wore their look of surprise.

- Joomla learners are of all ages. We've taught 15-year old students skipping class all the way up to retirees who are over 80.

If any of those descriptions sound like you, you've picked up the right book.

Using plain English and straightforward instructions, this book will help teach you how to build great websites using Joomla.

## THIS BOOK IS ACTIVE

You don't learn to ride a bicycle by reading a book: You learn by actually riding.

You don't learn to drive a car by reading a book: You learn by actually driving.

A book can help and give some advice, but without actually riding a bike or driving a car, you'll never really learn. The same is true with Joomla.

So throughout every chapter of this book, you're going to be asked to work with Joomla.

## THIS BOOK USES SPECIFIC EXAMPLES

After you master the techniques in this book, you can build your own websites for companies, charities, schools, sports, or whatever else you need.

However, this book uses a specific example site. Asking all the readers of this book to build the same site makes it easy for us to give you specific instructions, explanations, and screenshots.

It's not essential that you follow every task provided, but by following the flow of each chapter, you can get a good understanding of all the key Joomla concepts.

The example we're going to use is a website about Joomla. You're going to create a site with information about Joomla. The project is called Joomlaville. That's going to be the project you use to see how to build and run a Joomla site.

You can also find lots of extra information at http://ostraining.com/books/j3e.

## THIS BOOK WILL LEAVE SOME THINGS OUT

Big books are no fun. They're expensive to buy, heavy to carry, and often written in long, complicated sentences, paragraphs, and chapters that go on and on while the text grows and the words grow longer and more obscure as the author tries to show their verbosity and vocabulary, examining the thesaurus for words that describe, narrate, impress, and fill up space but never quite get to the point so that you end up going back to the beginning of the long confusing text and try to reread, but then you start wondering what's for dinner or what's on TV instead.

Yes, this book will also include some bad jokes.

This book is as small as possible because it leaves things out.

You're going to read that time and time again, but it's worth repeating: This book will leave things out.

You will focus on only the most important parts of Joomla so that you can understand them as easily as possible.

This book is not comprehensive. It does not contain everything you could know about Joomla. It contains only what a Joomla beginner needs to know.

## THIS BOOK USES ALMOST NO CODE

You do not need to know any HTML and CSS to use this book. That is a deliberate decision because we want to make this book accessible to ordinary people. We believe you don't have to be a developer to use Joomla.

However, that will disappoint some of you because this book does not discuss designing themes or building modules. If you do know CSS and PHP and want to dive into more advanced topics, there's a lot of advanced training at https://ostraining.com/classes/joomla.

## THINGS IN THIS BOOK WILL CHANGE

Joomla changes regularly, and so do the extra features and designs that you add on to it.

Everything in this book is correct at the time of writing. However, it's possible that some of the instructions and screen shots may become out-of-date.

Be patient with any changes you find. Email us at books@ostraining.com if you think any has changed. People do that all the time, and we include a big "Thank You!" to them in the next update of the book.

## WHAT YOU NEED FOR THIS BOOK

Now that you know a little bit about this book, let's make sure you're ready to follow along.

You need only two things to follow along with the exercises in this book:

- A computer with an Internet connection
- A hosting account or computer where you can install Joomla

Yes, that 's really all you need.

## ABOUT JOOMLASHACK

This book was made possible by the support of Joomlashack.

We use Joomlashack extensions and templates to power all our Joomla sites.

The Joomlashack team built some of the most popular Joomla extensions in the world, including these:

- **OSMap** is a sitemap extension and will improve your SEO by helping Google find your site's content.
- **JCal Pro** is an awesome Joomla events calendar.
- **OSEmbed** allows you to embed anything in Joomla! With only the URL, you can easily share Twitter, Facebook, Instagram and other content.
- **OSCampus** is the best way to build an online training site with Joomla.

Check them out at http://joomlashack.com.

## ABOUT THE OSTRAINING EVERYTHING CLUB

Joomla 3 Explained is part of the OSTraining Everything Club.

The club gives you access to all of the video classes, plus all the "Explained" books from OSTraining.

- These books are always up-to-date. Because we self-publish, we can release constant updates.

- These books are active. We don't do long, boring explanations.

- You don't need any experience. The books are suitable even for complete beginners.

Join the OSTraining Everything Club today by visiting our website at https://ostraining.com. You'll be able to download ebook copies of "Joomla 3 Explained" and all our other books and videos.

 OSTraining

## ABOUT THE OSTRAINING TEAM

---

I've split my career between teaching and web development. In 2007, I combined the two careers by starting to teach web development. Our company, OSTraining, now teaches Joomla classes around the world and online. I'm originally from England, and now live in Florida.

This book also would not be possible without the help of the OSTraining team.

Thanks to my wife, Stacey. She has saved me from many mistakes over the years, and many terrible typos in this book.

# WE OFTEN UPDATE THIS BOOK

This is version 2.3 of Joomla 3 Explained. This version was released on April 4, 2019.

We aim to keep this book up-to-date, and so will regularly release new versions to keep up with changes in Joomla.

Version 1.0 of this book was published by Pearson in July, 2014.

## ADVANTAGES AND DISADVANTAGES

We often release updates for this book. Most of the time, frequent updates are wonderful. If Joomla makes a change in the morning, we can have a new version of this book available in the afternoon. Most traditional publishers wait years and years before updating their books.

There are two disadvantages to be aware of:

- Page numbers do change. We often add and remove material from the book to reflect changes in Joomla.
- There's no index at the back of this book. This is because page numbers do change, and also because our self-publishing platform doesn't have a way to create indexes yet. We hope to find a solution for that soon.

Hopefully, you think that the advantages outweigh the disadvantages. If you have any questions, we're always happy to chat: books@ostraining.com.

## THANK YOU TO OUR READERS

If you find anything that is wrong or out-of-date, please email us at books@ostraining.com. We'll update the book, and to say thank you, we'll provide you with a new copy.

## ARE YOU AN AUTHOR?

If you enjoy writing about the web, we'd love to talk with you.

Most publishing companies are slow, boring, inflexible, and don't pay very well.

Here at OSTraining, we try to be different:

- **Fun**: We use modern publishing tools that make writing books as easy as blogging.
- **Fast**: We move quickly. Some books get written and published in less than a month.
- **Flexible**: It's easy to update your books. If technology changes in the morning, you can update your book by the afternoon.
- **Fair**: Profits from the books are shared 50/50 with the author.

Do you have a topic you'd love to write about? We publish books on almost all web-related topics.

Whether you want to write a short 100-page overview, or a comprehensive 500-page guide, we'd love to hear from you.

Contact us via email: books@ostraining.com.

# ARE YOU A TEACHER?

---

Many schools, colleges and organizations have adopted Joomla 3 Explained as a teaching guide.

This book is designed to be a step-by-step guide that students can follow at different speeds. The book can be used for a one-day class, or a longer class over multiple weeks.

If you are interested in teaching Joomla, we'd be delighted to help you with review copies, and all the advice you need.

Please email books@ostraining.com to talk with us.

Sample course outlines, descriptions, and learning outcomes are available at: https://ostraining.com/books/j3e/classroom.

# SPONSORING AN OSTRAINING BOOK

Is your company interested in sponsoring an OSTraining book?

Our books are some of the world's best-selling guides to the software they cover.

People love to read our books and learn about new web design topics.

Why not reach those people? Partner with us to showcase your company to thousands of web developers.

We have partnered with Acquia, Pantheon, Nexcess, GoDaddy, InMotion, GlowHost, and Ecwid to provide sponsored training to millions of people.

If you want to learn more, visit https://ostraining.com/ sponsor or email us at books@ostraining.com.

# WE WANT TO HEAR FROM YOU

Are you satisfied with your purchase of Joomla 3 Explained? Let us know and help us reach others who would benefit from this book.

We encourage you to share your experience. Here are two ways you can help:

- Leave your review on Amazon's product page of Joomla 3 Explained.

- Email your review to books@ostraining.com.

Thanks for reading Joomla 3 Explained. We wish you the best in your future endeavors with Joomla!

# THE LEGAL DETAILS

# JOOMLA 3 EXPLAINED

*Your Step-by-Step Guide to Joomla 3*

## STEPHEN BURGE

*OSTraining*

# CONTENTS

# CHAPTER 1.

# JOOMLA EXPLAINED

---

In this book, you're going to learn to build great Joomla websites.

Before you start, you probably need to know something about Joomla. This chapter is a brief introduction.

## WHERE DOES JOOMLA COME FROM?

Here's some of the key information you should know about Joomla:

- **What is Joomla?** It's web-publishing software. It's designed for people to publish content online: news, blogs, photos, products, documents, events, or 1001 other things. Because it allows you to manage your content, you'll often hear it called a Content Management System or CMS.

- **When did Joomla start?** Joomla has been around in various forms since 2000. Initially it was called Mambo, and in 2005 the name changed to Joomla.

- **Where did Joomla start?** It was created by Australians, which according to some people explains many of the quirks. It now has developers based all over the world with particularly strong representation coming from Europe, North America, South-east Asia and of course, Australia.

- **Who runs Joomla?** Joomla is run by volunteers. They are wonderful, kind-hearted people. However, they do still need to keep a roof over their heads and eat. Many of them have Joomla businesses in the day-time and volunteer in their spare time helping to keep the project running.

## WHY JOOMLA?

So why should you choose Joomla instead of many other options for building a website? Here are some of the best reasons:

- **It's easier**. I can't promise that your Joomla experience will be 100% frustration-free. There will be some moments when you're stuck and wish you'd taken up knitting instead. However, Joomla is much easier than most other types of website software and really there's not very much to learn. Once you've mastered the basics in this book, you can go out and build great Joomla sites.

- **It's quicker**. Joomla provides you with many ready-built features. If you want a new site design or to add a calendar or shopping cart to your site, you can often do it with just a few clicks. It may take a few days or even weeks to build a really great Joomla site, but you'll be able to develop and launch more quickly than with many alternatives.

- **It's cheaper**. Building a Joomla site is unlikely to be completely cost-free because at a certain point you may need to spend some money. You may have purchased this book or other training, and you might buy a new design or feature for your site. A good Joomla site may cost you between a few dollars and thousands of dollars at the top end. However, commercial alternatives to Joomla often cost tens or hundreds of thousands of dollars.

- **It has more options**. If you'd like extra features on your Joomla site, https://extensions.joomla.org is the place to go. It lists thousands of options. For example, if you'd like a calendar, there are around 20 options; and if you'd like a photo gallery, there are around 60 options. All of those numbers will have probably gone up by the time you read this, so there really are a lot of options. Though at some point you may have to hire a developer if you have very unusual or specific requirements. M,any of the things you'll need for your site have already been built.

## HOW MUCH IS JOOMLA?

Free. Yes, 100% free.

The software is free to use, free to download, free to use on your sites, free to use on your customers' sites.

There are also many free features available. You can find designs that people have created and are giving away. You can also find free shopping carts, calendars, photo galleries, and much more.

However, there are companies that make a living by selling products for Joomla. If you'd like a very impressive design or feature, there are companies that sell them, typically for a price between $5 and $150.

## WHAT DOES JOOMLA MEAN?

Yes, Joomla is a silly name. We admit it. Why was it chosen? Well, the domain name was available. OK, that sounds like a joke, but it's partially true. It was also chosen because the alternatives were so bad: they included Zegris and Feenix.

You might have guessed that Joomla isn't a real word. It's the phonetic spelling of a Swahili word "Jumla" which means "all together" or "as a whole."

The logo is shown in the image below:

It was chosen during a competition in 2005. The winning designer started with several letter "J"s for "Joomla" and rotated them until they fit together smoothly.

Adding the circles to each "J" gave the impression of people, and the multiple colors gave the impression of different races, people and cultures.

The Joomla logo has the same meaning as the name: people all together as one.

### HOW MANY VERSIONS OF JOOMLA ARE THERE?

At least two. We're going to be using version 3 in this book.

- **Joomla 2** was released in 2011.
- **Joomla 3** was released in 2012, and has been updated and improved many times since then.

In the future, more versions will be released. Don't let that put you off. New versions of Joomla are like the new versions of cars. This year's Toyota, Ford or Honda might have small improvements or tweaks over last year's model, but it's instantly recognizable as the same car and you'll have little problem moving from one to the other.

The key concepts of Joomla don't change, and in this book we're going to focus on those key concepts. After you're finished, you'll hopefully be able to pick up a site using any version and be able to successfully use it.

It really is like learning to drive. You learn to drive in one type of car, but once you understand how to do it, you'll be able to quickly adapt to driving any other type of car.

## WHO USES JOOMLA?

**Governments**: Joomla is used by many national and regional government sites. International organizations such as United Nations and the European Union use Joomla, and so do governments from the U.S.A., the U.K. and Portugal to Indonesia, Sri Lanka, and Mongolia. One example is https://www.casarosada.gob.ar, the official website for the president of Argentina, shown below:

**Corporations**: Joomla powers many business, entertainment and news websites and can handle large amounts of traffic. Businesses from Porsche to Danone to Ikea to General Electric have led their way in their use of Joomla. One great example is the car company Peugeot, whose Joomla site at https://www.peugeot.com is shown in the image below:

Many leading businesses use Joomla for building many sites in different countries. For example, Nintendo uses Joomla for sites targeted at several European countries, including https://nintendo.dk, https://nintendo.se, https://nintendo.no and https://nintendo.fi.

**Media**: Leading newspapers in Chile, Italy, Nigeria, the Philippines and many other countries use Joomla. One of the most popular entertainment sites in the Netherlands, https://npo3fm.nl, is built in Joomla, as seen below:

**Tourism and events**: Tourist destinations and attractions around the world use Joomla to show their best side to tourists. One prominent example is the Monaco Yacht Show, whose beautiful website is available in both English and French at http://monacoyachtshow.com. See the image below:

**Famous people**: Individuals often choose Joomla for their personal sites, and that includes many celebrities. Michael Phelps, the record-breaking swimmer, uses Joomla at http://michaelphelps.com:

WHAT'S NEXT?

In this chapter, you've learned some important information about Joomla.

Our next step is to plan our Joomla site. Are you ready? If you are, turn the page and we'll start making plans for our new Joomla site.

# CHAPTER 2.

# JOOMLA PLANNING EXPLAINED

---

Before you build any website, it's important to plan.

However, it's difficult for you to plan a Joomla site at the moment because you have little or no experience with Joomla.

So, in this chapter we're going to suggest some things you should plan for before you begin building a Joomla site.

We're also going to recommend a workflow that will help you carry out your plan successfully.

At the end of this chapter, you should be able to:

- Understand what's involved in a website plan
- Understand what's involved in a project management plan
- Understand what's involved in a development plan
- Understand what's involved in a maintenance plan
- Start to think about the website, project management, development, and maintenance plans for the site we'll build in this book

## JOOMLA SITE PLANNING EXPLAINED

Planning means different things to different people. Your role in the project, your experience, and your skills all influence your approach to planning.

- If you are a project manager, your thoughts might go directly to scheduling and budgets.

- If you are a designer, your first thoughts might lean more toward how each page of the site will look.

- If you are a content manager, content development workflows might come to mind followed quickly by how the content will be organized on the site.

- If you are a developer, your idea of a plan might be which development methodology you want to use or which strategies are best for implementing the design created by the designer.

There are many things to consider when you plan. For example, if the schedule is tight and the budget is low, the planned design might not be possible. To take another example, if you do not have the appropriate skills on your development team, you might need to change your development strategy to one that meets most of your planned design, leaving the more customized functionality to a time when time, skills, and budget allow.

There are general guidelines, but each plan must be customized to your situation.

To plan a Joomla site, you need four types of plans:

1. Website
2. Project Management
3. Development
4. Maintenance

Now consider a brief introduction of each type of plan.

# 1. Website Plan

This plan focuses on defining the content and functional requirements, as well as the design (visual, structural, layout, and interaction) aspects of the site. The website plan conveys what you want for your site after it is built. It influences the schedule, required budget, and skills, and provides a way to manage expectations for all involved. The more detailed the plan, the higher probability that you will get the site you want, assuming all things equal.

A website plan commonly includes a requirements document and a design document.

The requirements document includes but is not limited to the:

- Types of content required
- Communication strategies the site needs to support
- Strategies that will support visitors finding the content they need
- Features that add value to the users' experiences
- Roles of your users and what they will be allowed to do
- Performance expectations based on the projected use
- Security requirements

The design document includes but is not limited to the:

- Wireframes for the homepage, the landing pages, and the different types of content
- Interaction plan describing the behavior of the objects included in the wireframes
- Style guide to be used when rendering the visual aspects of the site

- Theme region plan required to support the layout strategies assumed in the wireframes
- Graphic rendering of the finished pages

## 2. Project Management Plan

For this type of plan, you should consider the resources required to meet the website plan and the maintenance plan:

- What skills will you need?
- What order will the website planning and development tasks be accomplished?
- When can the site be launched?
- How much will it cost?
- How will you monitor progress?
- How will you manage expectations if a requirement or design feature cannot be met as originally requested?

These are only some of the questions that fall into the realm of project management. With these questions, you can start a discussion with those involved in the website project, whether you are the client, the developer, or the designer.

The project management plan can include one or more of the following:

- Schedule
- Budget
- Skills
- Expectations

## 3. Development Plan

Development plans are a source of much discussion among

people who build websites. As you've seen, a simple development plan could be this: Install Joomla.

For professionals, entire methodologies have grown up around development plans. Two of the most famous are Agile and Waterfall.

The development plan can document your content strategy. For example, if you add events to your site, you can enter all the event information into one text field or split the information into different fields, such as date, location, and price.

What would influence your decision? For a simple site, it might be sufficient to have all the information in one text field. For a larger, more complex site you may need to filter or sort events by date, location, price, host, and more. To filter and sort in this way, you need to make sure that information is entered into different fields.

Another aspect of a development plan is when each strategy will be implemented. For instance, will each section of the site be implemented one at a time? Or will aspects of each site section be implemented, thus implementing all sections at the same time but in varying degrees of detail?

In the end, the development plan should convey what is needed to implement the requirements and design in the website plan and meet the project management expectations regarding schedule and budget. For example, development plans can include one or more of the following:

- A list of different types of content along with their data fields, features, and user permissions
- A list of features needed on your site together with the modules required to provide those features
- A strategy for the design of your site

- A development methodology
- A test plan that covers each aspect of testing, including integration, regression, security, usability, and accessibility

### 4. Maintenance Plan

Maintenance tasks are typically performed after the site is officially launched, but that doesn't mean you start planning your maintenance when the site is about to go live. At least three types of maintenance tasks need to be planned:

- Routine monitoring maintenance
- Planned update maintenance
- Site management

The way you plan to perform each type of maintenance can influence development strategies. For instance, if you plan to maintain the content on your site by allowing particular people to manage specific types of content, the development team needs to be aware of that and provide the necessary functionality.

### OUR JOOMLAVILLE WEBSITE PLAN

As mentioned in the previous chapter, we're going to build a site called Joomlaville. By the end of this book, our plan is for the site to look like the image below:

## Our Joomlaville Content Requirements

The site we're going to build in this book has multiple types of content. Here's a list of the types of content that we'll add to our site:

- Information about Joomlaville
- Attractions
- Transport
- Parks
- News from other Joomla sites

## Our Joomlaville Communications Requirements

The site we're going to build will also have these types of communication:

- The content communicates the message.

- Social media links provided can help visitors share pages of the site with others.
- Contact forms will allow users to reach the administrators on the site.

## Our Joomlaville Navigation Requirements

We're going to provide the following to help visitors navigate the site:

- Menus
- Dynamically generated lists of content
- Breadcrumbs

## Our Joomlaville Feature Requirements

Other additional features are needed to improve the functionality for our Joomlaville site:

- Social sharing capability
- Login forms
- Contact forms
- Search
- Site map

## Our Joomlaville User Requirements

There will be several different groups of users:

- Anonymous visitors who can only look at the site
- Authenticated users who can log in
- Park writers who can manages the Parks listings
- Administrators who have free reign to do anything on the site

## Our Joomlaville Design Requirements

To help you visualize what our Joomlaville site can look like at the end of this book, here are some landing pages you will be building:

- Information articles: These will be displayed in a teaser list layout with comments and social media links, as shown below:

- News articles: These will be displayed in a blog layout and will pull in content from other Joomla sites, as shown below:

## Our Joomlaville Project Management Plan

Project management plans aren't usually conveyed in four bullet points, but here is a quick summary of what we'll need to complete this book's project successfully:

- **Schedule:** You'll build this site at your own pace. Someone working quickly may finish this book in two days or less. Someone without so much free time can build the site successfully, but more slowly.

- **Budget:** Zero. You won't need to spend any money to build the site for this book.

- **Skills:** Zero. You'll learn everything you need to know to build the site.

- **Expectations:** Your first Joomla site does not come with very complicated expectations. Your Joomlaville site won't be the most beautiful Joomla site in the world, and it won't make you a million dollars. However, we do expect that it will be a giant step towards helping you learn Joomla.

## Our Joomlaville Development Plan

Here is the order in which we're going to tackle the development of our site. This book does follow the order of this plan:

- Content
- Fields
- Menus
- Extensions (Components, Modules, Plugins)
- Templates
- Users
- Site Management

## Our Joomlaville Maintenance Plan

Because the site we're creating in this book is only designed to help you learn, we don't necessarily need an ongoing maintenance plan. At the end of this book, you have two options:

- You can delete the Joomlaville site that we've built.
- You can maintain the Joomlaville site using the techniques shown in the final chapter, "Joomla Site Maintenance Explained".

### WHAT'S NEXT?

Now that we've discussed planning, you're ready to build your first Joomla site.

Turn the page and let's continue with the next step in our Joomla plan: installation.

# CHAPTER 3.

## JOOMLA INSTALLATIONS EXPLAINED

---

This chapter will show you where and how to install Joomla. When you've finished, you should have a complete Joomla site. That is where you can practice everything else we'll be doing in this book.

After reading this chapter, you'll be able to do the following:

- Choose the best place to install Joomla
- Choose the best way to install Joomla
- Install Joomla on launch.joomla.org
- Install Joomla automatically
- Install Joomla manually
- Get help if you're stuck with installing Joomla

### CHOOSING THE BEST PLACE TO INSTALL JOOMLA

Joomla is not like many other software programs. It can't just run on any computer. It requires a server in order to run successfully. That means you normally have the choice of installing Joomla in one of two places:

- A local server installed on your computer
- A web server

Choosing the best place to install Joomla is important, so here is an explanation of the difference between the two options.

## Your Computer

There are several useful advantages to working on your computer:

- **Working offline:** You can work without an internet connection.
- **Privacy:** Your Joomla site will be safe and private, accessible only to people who can access that computer.
- **Free:** There are no fees to pay.

However, there are also several important disadvantages to using a computer:

- **Extra installations needed:** You need to download and configure special software for your computer.
- **Difficult to get help:** You can't easily show it to other people and ask for help.
- **Only one computer:** You can only access it from the computer you used to install it.
- **Need to move in order to launch:** When you're ready to make your site public, you'll need to move everything to a web server and adjust for any differences between the two locations.

Because of these disadvantages, installing on your computer can present significant obstacles for a beginner. I'm going to recommend that you don't take this route until you have more experience.

## A Web Server

Unlike your computer, a web server is specifically designed for hosting websites so they are easy to visit for anyone who's online.

If you work for a company, they may be able to provide a server. However, for most of us we'll need to rent space from a hosting company. There are two common types of web servers, Linux and Microsoft. Both require PHP, because that is the language Joomla is written in, and MySQL, because it is the type of database Joomla uses. These are the minimum versions recommended:

- **PHP**: 5.6 or above.
- **MySQL**: 5.5.3 or above.

Linux servers also require Apache, a type of web server software. The minimum version for that is 2 and above.

When it comes to choosing a server, Apache has long been the favorite choice for running Joomla. Microsoft is working hard to make Joomla run as smoothly as possible on their servers, but for now, Apache is still my recommendation.

Most hosting companies support Joomla, but it's worth choosing carefully. Some hosting companies are much better than others. Here is some advice before picking your host:

- Search http://forum.joomla.org for other people's experiences with that host.

- Contact their customer support and ask them what they know about Joomla. One of our training students actually called the phone numbers of several hosts and timed their responses. After all, in an emergency you don't want to be on hold for an hour or talking to someone who knows nothing about Joomla.

- Check prices. Most good hosting companies will charge around $6 to $10 per month for approximately 1 GB of space (enough for a 2000 page site) and 50 GB of bandwidth (enough for about 100,000 visitors per month).

## THE BEST WAY TO INSTALL JOOMLA ON A WEB SERVER

For people who choose to install Joomla on a web server, there are three common ways to install Joomla:

1. Use launch.joomla.org.
2. Use a "One-Click" installation.
3. Upload the files and create the database manually.

launch.joomla.org is the option that we recommend for most people. This is the official hosting site of the Joomla project. This hosting is completely free, so long as you log in and click a "renew" button once every 30 days.

The "One-Click" installation method is another reliable and easy way to install Joomla, but you do need to make sure it is supported by your hosting company.

If you choose to install Joomla manually, you'll be moving Joomla files to the web server. For that we'll need FTP (File Transfer Protocol) software. One good choice is Filezilla, which is free to download and can work on Windows, Mac, or Linux computers. To download it, go to http://filezilla-project.org and click on "Download Filezilla Client".

In this next part of the this chapter, we're going to show you all three ways to install Joomla.

## OPTION #1. LAUNCH.JOOMLA.ORG

This is the fastest and easiest way to get up-and-running for this book.

- Go to launch.joomla.org.

- Enter a Site Name. Unfortunately, I've already chosen Joomlaville, so you will need a different name.

- Enter your email address.

- Check the box, "I agree to the Terms of Service and Privacy Policy."

- Click "Launch now".

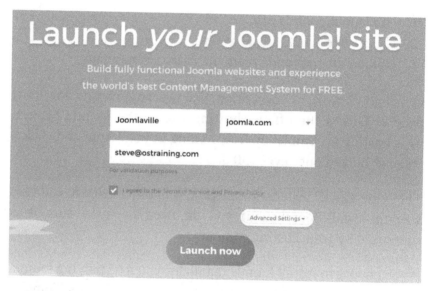

- You'll see a "Ready for Launch!" page. There's also a link here to the official Joomla training videos ... provided by OSTraining, of course!

# Ready for Launch!

Next Step: Check your email

Please check your email for a validation link that will launch your site. Once launched, you will receive a second email with login details to your new Joomla site.

Learn Joomla with free video training →

- Check your email inbox for the link to your new site.
- Click the verification link inside this email.

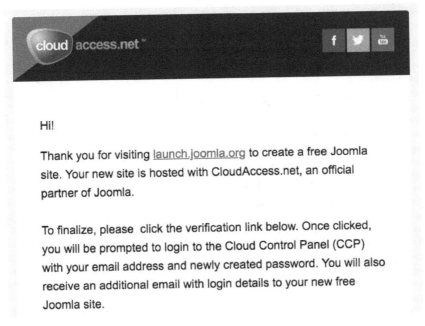

Hi!

Thank you for visiting launch.joomla.org to create a free Joomla site. Your new site is hosted with CloudAccess.net, an official partner of Joomla.

To finalize, please click the verification link below. Once clicked, you will be prompted to login to the Cloud Control Panel (CCP) with your email address and newly created password. You will also receive an additional email with login details to your new free Joomla site.

- After confirming your email, you'll get the username and password for your new site.

Hi Joomla User,

Thank you for launching a free Joomla website! Your free Joomla site is hosted with CloudAccess.net, an official partner of Joomla, and an industry leader in Joomla hosting and support. Follow the steps below to access your site to begin learning and building today!

### Step 1: Access your Joomla! Site

Your Joomla site is now active at http://alledia._____.joomla.com . You have two options for accessing the administration area (the back end) of your Joomla site where you'll create and manage all of the site's content, users, media and more.

**Option #1:** Log into the site manually by going to http://alledia._____.joomla.com/administrator/ and using the login details below.

**Login Details:**
Username: celoweyi
Password: z1WZRHKi

- Log into your Joomla site administrator area using the details in your email.

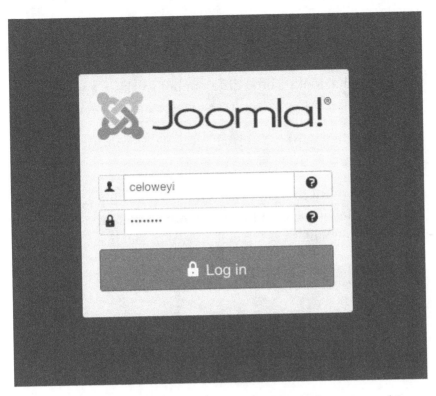

- You'll now be logged in to your new site! If you can see this screen, you're ready to move on to the next chapter!

## OPTION #2. INSTALLING JOOMLA AUTOMATICALLY

Automatic installers are often called "One Click" installers. To tell you the truth, "One Click" is a small exaggeration. Installing Joomla this way really takes about five clicks.

There are many different versions of "One Click" installers. We're going to use one of the most popular installers, which is called "Softaculous." Your hosting company may offer an alternative that looks a little different but works in a very similar way. The two most popular alternatives are cPanel and Plesk.

Here are the steps to install Joomla automatically using Softaculous:

- Log into your web hosting account. Each hosting account will look a little different, but there are often similarities. Many hosting companies use CPanel, shown in the image below:

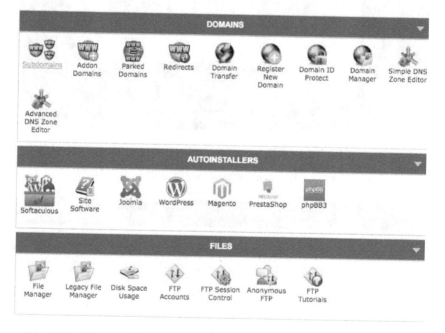

- Find the "Joomla" button and click it. The button may be found on any of the rows, but you can normally find it by looking for the Joomla logo, as shown below. If you can't see the Joomla logo, look for the "Softaculous" name or a link which says "Automatic Installers".

- After clicking on the Joomla button, you'll be taken to the main Softaculous screen for Joomla. Your screen should look similar to the one shown in the image below. Click on "Install" at the top:

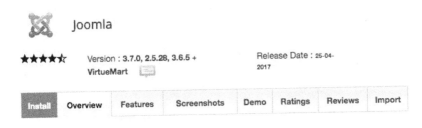

Enter your new site settings. Softaculous will now ask for the details of your new site. The options are shown in the figure below. Here's what you need to know:

- **Choose the version you want to install**: Leave this as it is, on the highest possible version number.

- **Choose Protocol**: Leave this as it is, with no additional security settings.

- **Choose domain**: Leave this as it is. This will be the main domain name where your site is installed.

- **Install in directory**: You can leave this blank if you'd like the site to be accessible directly via your domain, for example: http://www.ostraining.com. The alternative that I'm going to recommend for learning with this book is to use a sub-folder.

For example, as we're building a site about Joomlaville, we can place the site at http://www.ostraining.com/joomlaville/. If you do this, it's not difficult to move your site if you later want to make it accessible directly via your domain. So, go ahead and enter "joomlaville" into this field:

Software Setup

| | |
|---|---|
| Choose the version you want to install | 3.7.0 |
| Please select the version to install. | |
| Choose Protocol | https:// |
| If your site has SSL, then please choose the HTTPS protocol. | |
| Choose Domain | ostraining. |
| Please choose the domain to install the software. | |
| In Directory | joomlaville |
| The directory is relative to your | |

- **Site Name**: Enter "Joomlaville" here. This name will appear at the top of your new site.

- **Site Description**: Enter "A great place to learn Joomla".

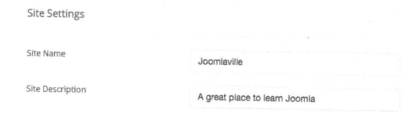

Site Settings

| | |
|---|---|
| Site Name | Joomlaville |
| Site Description | A great place to learn Joomla |

- **Import Sample Data**: Choose "Default" English". This will give us a site that is immediately ready to use.

Database Settings

| Import Sample Data<br>*(In order to have the SiteGround sample<br>data preinstalled leave the sample data<br>check box selected.)* | Default English (GB) ⬍ |
| --- | --- |

- **Admin Username**: Enter the username you want to use when you log into your site.

- **Admin Password**. This is the password you'll use to log in to your site. Please don't use "admin" here! Don't use "password", "1234" or "iloveyou" either. A good combination of numbers, punctuation and uppercase and lowercase letters is vital.

- **Real name**: Enter your own name.

- **Admin Email**: Enter your email address.

Admin Account

| Admin Username | steve | |
| --- | --- | --- |
| Admin Password | #ELWIO1S&& | **Hide** |
| | Strong (60/100) | |
| Real Name | Steve Burge | |
| Admin Email | steve@ostraining.com | |

- Once you've entered all your information and clicked "Install," you'll see a progress bar like the one below:

Checking the submitted data (9 %)

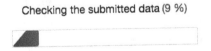

**NOTE:** This may take 3-4 minutes. Please do not leave this page until the progress bar reaches 100%

- You'll now be taken to the final Joomla screen in Softaculous. Your installation has been completed. There will be two links:

  ○ The full URL to this installation of Joomla

  ○ The full URL to the administrator area

Bookmark both of these links in your browser. You'll be using both of these links often!

- **Visit your new site:** Go ahead and click the URL to this installation of Joomla link. You'll now see a new website like the image below:

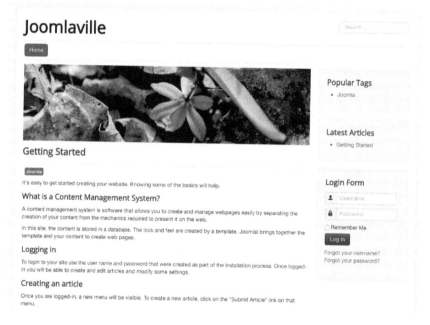

- Try logging into your new site. You can log into your site by typing in the location of your site and then the word /administrator/ at the end. So in the example you saw above, the login area is at http://ostraining.com/joomlaville/ administrator. If you're in the right place, you'll see a login screen like the one in the figure below. Log in using the username and password you created earlier.

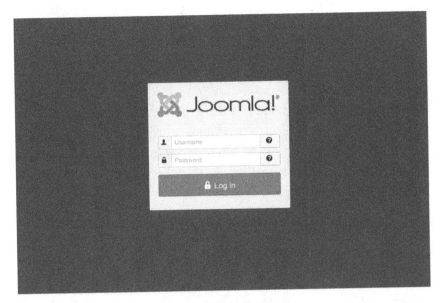

- View the Joomla Control Panel. If you remembered your username and password correctly, you'll be taken to the main control panel for your Joomla site. It will look like the image displayed below:

Congratulations! You can now go straight to the end of this chapter! Most of the rest of this chapter will be spent installing Joomla manually, but even many experienced Joomla users prefer to do things automatically using a "One Click" installer.

An old-fashioned HTML website consists only of one part: files. It doesn't need anything else to run.

However, a Joomla website is a little different because it consists not only of files but also a database to store all the site's information. We're going to have to set-up both the files and the database, then connect them together. So, the process of installing Joomla manually is this:

- Step #1: Create a database
- Step #2: Download the Joomla files and upload them to our web server
- Step #3: Complete the Joomla installation by connecting the database and files together

**Step #1: Create a Database**

Our first step will be to create a database to store all the unique information about our site.

A database is basically a group of tables with letters and numbers stored in its rows and columns. Think of it as several spreadsheets. There's a spreadsheet with all of the articles you write. There's another for all of the users who register on your site. The database makes it easy for Joomla to easily handle large amounts of data. If a new article or user is added, Joomla just needs to add an extra row to the appropriate spreadsheet. Joomla uses a particular type of database known as MySQL.

Let's go ahead and set up a database for our new Joomla site:

- Log into your web hosting account. In this example, we're using a web hosting control panel called cPanel, as provided by a hosting company called Siteground.com. Their version of cPanel looks like the image below. Your hosting company may offer a slightly different version of cPanel, or they may offer an alternative that looks a little different but works in a very similar way.

- Find the button that says "MySQL Databases" (as seen on the far left of the screen below) and click it. The button may be on any of the rows, but you can normally spot it by looking for the MySQL name and the blue dolphin logo.

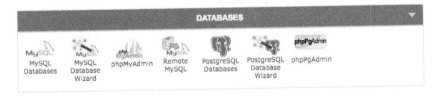

- Enter a name that is relatively easy to remember and click "Create Database". Be sure to write this name down, and note that it's likely to have your hosting account name before it. In the image below, our new database will be called ostrain2_joomlaville.

**Create a New Database**

New Database: ostrain2_ joomlaville

Create Database

Next, we create a user account so that we can access the database. Without password protection, anyone might be able to log in and see our site's important information. Here's what you need to do:

- Choose a username. Enter a short username here, different from anything you've used before. In this example, I'm using "joomlav". The username is a little confusing because our hosting account name is added also, so in the image below, our full username will be ostrain2_joomlav.

- Choose a password. Some versions of cPanel will help you choose a password that is very difficult to guess. If you set your own choice, please use a combination of numbers, punctuation and uppercase and lowercase letters so that the password is hard to guess.

- Be sure to record both your username and password safely. We're going to need them again very soon.

- Click "Create User". You should see a message saying the user has been created successfully.

**MySQL Users**

**Add a New User**

Username: ostrain2_ |joomlav        ✓

Password: •••••••••••••••••        ✓

Password (Again): •••••••••••••••••        ✓

Strength (Why?):  | Very Strong (100/100) |  | Password Generator |

| Create a User |

Now we need to allow our new user to be able to login to the database.

- Find the area called "Add User To Database".

- Choose your database name and then your username before clicking "Add".

**Add a User to a Database**

User:  | ostrain2_joomlav ⬍ |

Database:  | ostrain2_joomlaville ⬍ |

| Add |

- The final step in this process is to decide what our new user can and cannot do with the database. As in the image below, we're going to give them "All" permissions so that our Joomla site can make whatever changes it needs to the database. Click on "Make Changes"" to finish the process:

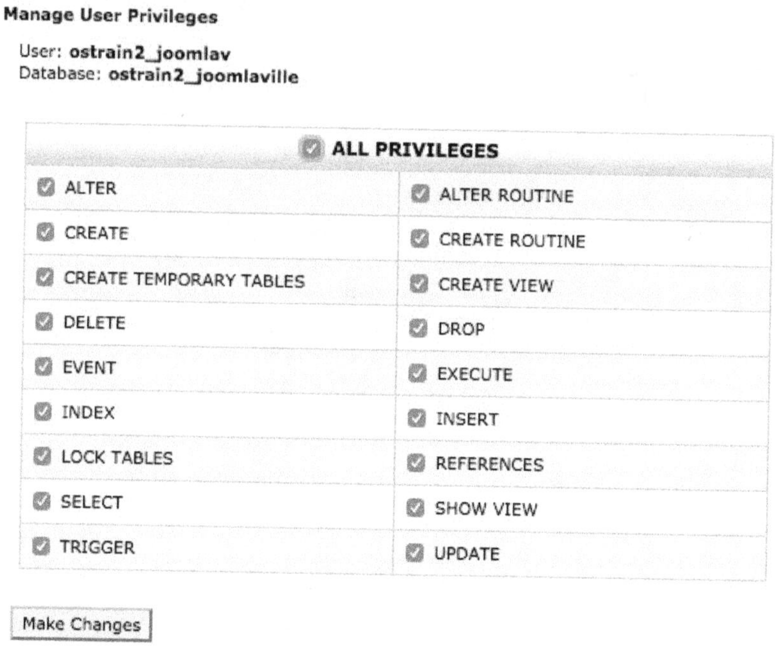

**Manage User Privileges**

User: **ostrain2_joomlav**
Database: **ostrain2_joomlaville**

| ☑ **ALL PRIVILEGES** | |
|---|---|
| ☑ ALTER | ☑ ALTER ROUTINE |
| ☑ CREATE | ☑ CREATE ROUTINE |
| ☑ CREATE TEMPORARY TABLES | ☑ CREATE VIEW |
| ☑ DELETE | ☑ DROP |
| ☑ EVENT | ☑ EXECUTE |
| ☑ INDEX | ☑ INSERT |
| ☑ LOCK TABLES | ☑ REFERENCES |
| ☑ SELECT | ☑ SHOW VIEW |
| ☑ TRIGGER | ☑ UPDATE |

Make Changes

## Step #2: Download the Joomla Files

Now that we have the database ready, we're going to download the Joomla files. These contain all of the code and images that Joomla needs to run.

- Go to http://joomla.org and click on the button saying "Download Joomla!"

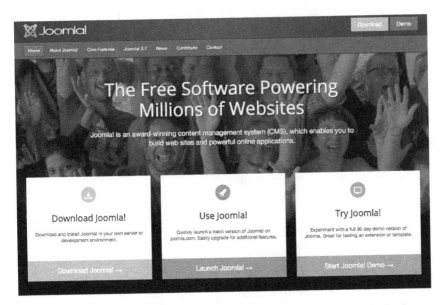

- You'll now see a page with several download links. Click the "Download Joomla!" button on the left.

- After clicking the download link, you'll receive a .zip file with a name like this: Joomla_3.7.2-Stable-Full_Package.zip. It contains all the files you'll need to install Joomla.

- Now you need to uncompress the .zip file. On a Windows computer, you can right-click on the file and choose "Extract Here". On a Mac, if the file doesn't unzip automatically, you can click on "File" then "Open With" and choose "Archive Utility". The folder will have a name similar to Joomla_3.7.2-Stable-Full_Package. Right-click on the folder and rename it to /joomlaville/.

- Open the folder, and the contents will look like this:

We're now going to start the process of moving our files on to our web server.

- The first step is to open your FTP software such as Filezilla. Then log in to your FTP account and browse to the folder where you want to install Joomla. Often this will be the root directory, which often has a name such as /public_html/, /www/ or /htdocs/.

- Select the folder that you just downloaded, extracted and renamed. Move this folder via your FTP software into the folder where you're installing Joomla. With Filezilla this is as simple as dragging-and-dropping the files. Uploading might take from 5 to 30 minutes or more depending on the speed of your internet connection.

## Step #3: Complete the Joomla Installation

We've now successfully set up the two halves of our Joomla site: the database (Step #1) and the files (Step #2). Our final step is to connect those two halves together.

- Start your browser and visit the URL where you uploaded the files. In the example I've been using, that was to http://ostraining.com/joomlaville/.

- You should see an installation screen like the figure below. This is the first step in Joomla's easy-to-use installation manager.

Enter the information listed here, and then click the "Next" button:

- Site Name: **Joomlaville**
- Description: **A great place to learn Joomla.**
- Admin Email: Enter your email address.
- Admin Username: Enter the username you want to use when you log in to your site.
- Admin Password: This is the password you'll use to log in. Please don't use "admin" here also! Don't use "password", "1234" or "iloveyou" either. A good combination of numbers, punctuation and uppercase and lowercase letters is vital.

After clicking "Next" you will be asked for your database details. This is where you connect your files and database together. We're going to need the details we collected when we created the database earlier. Enter the information we list here, and then click the "Next" button.

- Username: Enter the details you collected earlier.
- Password: Enter the details you collected earlier.
- Database Name: Enter the details you collected earlier.

- You have almost finished the installation process. We just need to choose a few, final settings. First, let's install some sample data so that our site is ready to use straight away. In the options below, choose "Default English", as shown in the image below:

This step also verifies whether your hosting account is correctly set up to run Joomla. Scroll down and you'll see a screen like the one in the image below. If items are marked in green, then they're fine. However, if items are marked with red or yellow, you may need to fix them. The items at the top are essential, and Joomla can't run unless they're green. The items at the bottom are recommended but not essential: Joomla will still run if they're red.

What do you do if items are red? The bad news is that you can't fix many of these problems, even if you were a geek genius, because many hosting companies won't give you access. The good news is that the solution is easy: Copy-and-paste the items in red into a support ticket and ask your hosting company to fix them.

When the essential settings are green, click "Install" to move on.

### Pre-Installation Check

If any of these items are not supported (marked as No) then please take actions to correct them.
You can't install Joomla! until your setup meets the requirements below.

| | |
|---|---|
| PHP Version >= 5.3.10 | Yes |
| Magic Quotes GPC Off | Yes |
| Register Globals Off | Yes |
| Zlib Compression Support | Yes |
| XML Support | Yes |
| Database Support: (sqlite, pdo, pdomysql, postgresql, mysqli) | Yes |
| MB Language is Default | Yes |
| MB String Overload Off | Yes |
| INI Parser Support | Yes |
| JSON Support | Yes |
| Mcrypt Support | Yes |
| configuration.php Writeable | Yes |

### Recommended settings:

These settings are recommended for PHP in order to ensure full compatibility with Joomla.
However, Joomla! will still operate if your settings do not quite match the recommended configuration.

| Directive | Recommended | Actual |
|---|---|---|
| Safe Mode | Off | Off |
| Display Errors | Off | On |
| File Uploads | On | On |
| Magic Quotes Runtime | Off | Off |
| Output Buffering | Off | Off |
| Session Auto Start | Off | Off |
| Native ZIP support | On | On |

- You'll now see a message saying "Congratulations! Joomla! is now installed", as shown below:

Joomla! is free software released under the GNU General Public License.

**Congratulations! Joomla! is now installed.**

**Joomla! in your own language and/or automatic basic native multilingual site creation**

Before removing the installation folder you can install extra languages. If you want to add extra languages to your Joomla! application select the following button.

> Note: you will need internet access for Joomla! to download and install the new languages.
> Some server configurations won't allow Joomla! to install the languages. If this is your case, don't worry, you will be able to install them later using the Joomla! Administrator.

→ Extra steps: Install languages

PLEASE REMEMBER TO COMPLETELY REMOVE THE INSTALLATION FOLDER.
You will not be able to proceed beyond this point until the installation folder has been removed. This is a security feature of Joomla!

Remove installation folder

⊕ Site   🔒 Administrator

**Administration Login Details**

Email       steve@ostraining.com
Username    steve

- There is one final thing you must now do: click the button marked "Remove installation folder", as shown on the screen above. This is a security feature that will remove the code you just used to install Joomla and will stop anyone else from using it. After you've removed the installation folder, you'll see a screen like the one below:

**Congratulations! Joomla! is now installed.**

PLEASE REMEMBER TO COMPLETELY REMOVE THE INSTALLATION FOLDER.
You will not be able to proceed beyond this point until the installation folder has been removed. This is a security feature of Joomla!

Installation folder successfully removed.

⊕ Site   🔒 Administrator

**Administration Login Details**

Email       steve@ostraining.com
Username    steve

- Go ahead and click the "Site" button, which is located to next to the Administrator button.

- You'll now see a new website like the image below:

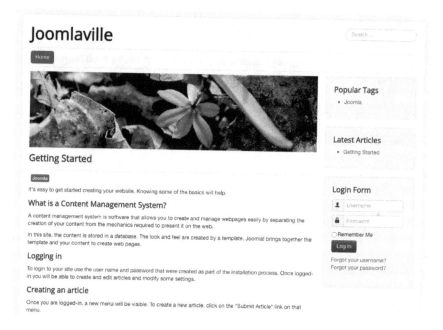

- Try logging into your new site. You can log into your site by typing in the location of your site and then the word /administrator/ at the end. So in the example you saw above, the login area is at http://ostraining.com/joomlaville/ administrator. If you're in the right place, you'll see a login screen like the one in the figure below. Log in using the username and password you created earlier.

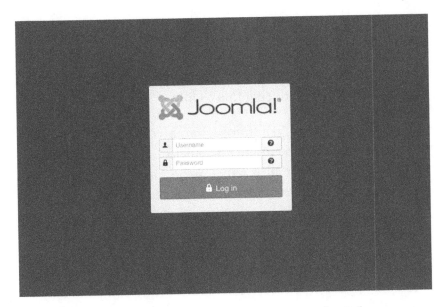

- View the Joomla Control Panel. If you remembered your username and password correctly, you'll be taken to the main control panel for your Joomla site. It will look like the image displayed below. If you can see this screen, you're ready to move onto the next chapter!

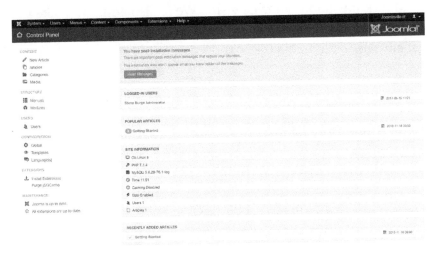

## GETTING HELP IF YOU'RE STUCK WITH INSTALLING JOOMLA

There are three places that I'd recommend going for help if you get stuck at any point during this chapter:

- **The Joomla Forum**: It's almost guaranteed that someone has experienced the same Joomla installation problem as you and has asked about it on http://forum.joomla.org. It's a great place to search for solutions and ask for help.

- **The Joomla help site**. There's an installation manual available for Joomla at http://docs.joomla.org.

- **Your hosting company**. If you see a specific error, it might be related to your web server, and your hosting company may be able to help.

## WHAT'S NEXT?

You now have a Joomla site ready to use. In the next chapter, we're going to introduce you to the most important things you need to know about your new site. We're also going to make the first changes to the site. Are you ready? Turn the page, and let's get started.

# CHAPTER 4.

## JOOMLA SITES EXPLAINED

This chapter explains the basic concepts of your Joomla site. After you've finished this chapter, you'll understand how users see your site and how administrators manage your site.

After reading this chapter, you'll be able to do the following:

- Understand the two areas of your Joomla site
- Understand the visitor area of your Joomla site
- Understand the administrator area of your Joomla site
- Make your first Joomla site changes

### UNDERSTANDING THE TWO AREAS OF A JOOMLA SITE

Every Joomla Web site has two areas: a public area for visitors and a private area for administrators.

### Visitor Area

Absolutely everything you want visitors to see on your site can be accessed from here.

You can always access the visitor area simply by visiting the Web address where you installed Joomla. Type in the Web address, and you should see a screen that looks like the image below:

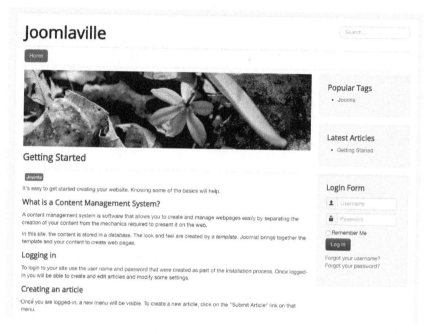

## Administrator Area

The other half of your Joomla site is the private area for administrators. Absolutely everything you want to change about your site can be changed from here. It is the Control Panel of your site, where you go to add content, create navigation, or modify your site layout.

This area is always accessible by adding /administrator to your site's home page. So if your site was http://ostraining.com/joomlaville, you'd add /administrator to visit the administrator area, and the URL would be http://ostraining.com/joomlaville/administrator.

If you haven't already logged in, enter the username and password that you created in Chapter 3, "Joomla Installations Explained", during the final stages of installing your site.

If you've lost those details already, click either "Forgot your username?" or "Forgot your password?" on the right-hand side.

Once you've logged in, you are taken to a screen looking like the image below. This is your top secret headquarters. This is the main Control Panel for your entire site. Absolutely everything you want to change about your site can be changed from here.

In this chapter, you get an overview of both areas of your Joomla site, and we start right here in the administrator area.

## UNDERSTAND THE ADMINISTRATOR AREA OF YOUR JOOMLA SITE

On every page your administrator area of your Joomla site, you'll see a dropdown menu that's shown below. This menu has all the key links you need to manage your site:

On the first screen you see after logging in, you'll see these quick links in the left sidebar. These links allow you to easily access the most important features in your administrator area:

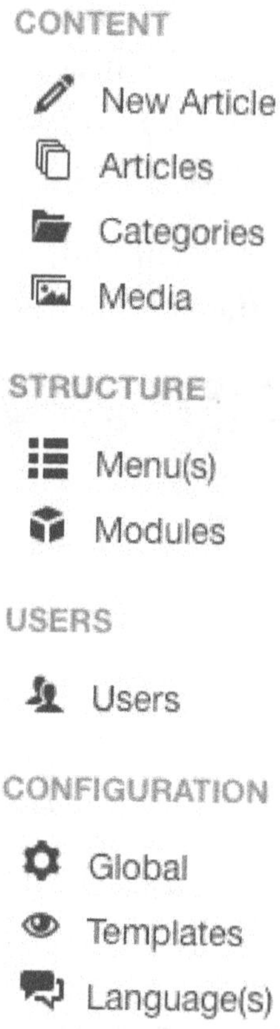

**CONTENT**

✏️ New Article

📑 Articles

📁 Categories

🖼️ Media

**STRUCTURE**

☰ Menu(s)

📦 Modules

**USERS**

👥 Users

**CONFIGURATION**

⚙️ Global

👁️ Templates

💬 Language(s)

The main area of the page includes key information about what's happening on your site:

I recommend that, as a beginner, you focus all your attention on the dropdown menu.

We use that dropdown menu to manage every aspect of our Joomla site. The quick links, short-cuts, and latest updates are all just other ways of getting to the same place.

Hover your mouse over the dropdown menu, and you'll see dropdown links, as in the image below:

Because the dropdown menu is so important, we base this entire book on it. Every time we ask you to visit a page in the administrator area, we go via this dropdown menu. The dropdown menu contains the following options:

- **System** contains all the main configuration options for your site. The good news is that most of these configuration options will be set up correctly when you first install your site.

- **Users** is where you can give different permissions to different users and groups of users. For example, if you are running a school Web site, you could decide that the history teacher could only write articles about history, the science teacher could only write about science, and the sports teacher could only enter game results.

- **Menus** contains the navigation for your visitors. Remember the menu links you were clicking on in the visitor area of the site? We can control and create these from this area.

- **Content** contains all of your text articles. Any text that you write goes here, from news and blog posts to essays and book chapters.

- **Components** are the powerful extra features you can add to your site. Social networking, photo galleries, shopping carts, event calendars, and much more are all called components.

- **Extensions** are the extra features you can add to your site. The Extensions dropdown menu includes links to the following types of extension:

  ○ **Modules.** Modules are the small little boxes around the outside of your site. They show visitors little snippets of information, such as the latest or most popular five articles.

  ○ **Plug-ins.** Plug-ins are tiny little scripts that make small improvements to your site. One example of a plug-in adds a small row of stars to the top of articles so that visitors can vote on articles. Another example loads a small piece of code to protect e-mail addresses from spammers.

- Templates. Templates are the design and layout of your site. If you want a red, blue, pink, green, yellow, white, or orange site, you need to find a template of the right color. If you want a particular site layout, you need to find a template with the right layout

- Languages. Joomla has been translated into more than 40 languages. You can upload Spanish, French, German, Japanese, Arabic, and many other languages. All Joomla's site functions will be automatically translated. However, you still need to manually translate any articles you write, as Joomla isn't that clever unfortunately.

• **Help** provides answers to your questions. I hope this book is useful, but you're certain to have more questions that we can't answer here. The Joomla Help link leads to documentation that you can view inside your site. The other links take you to the most important parts of the official Joomla site, http://joomla.org.

## THINGS YOU'LL SEE ALL THE TIME IN JOOMLA

It's confusing when things change. The good news is that Joomla is good at keeping things consistent. There are many things that you'll see all the time in Joomla. The following sections discuss some examples.

### Page Layouts

Joomla also uses similar layouts for every page you visit from the dropdown menu. For example, take a look at Joomla's Article Manager by clicking on Content and then on "Articles", as in the image below:

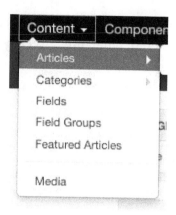

You'll now see the following screen shown below:

We've marked five features that are consistent on many Joomla pages.

1. **Page title.** This tells you where you are in your administrator area
2. **Action buttons.** These buttons allow you to modify any of the items you see.
3. **Submenu.** These links give you access to important, related parts of your administrator area.
4. **Search.** These search options allow you to quickly find what you're looking for.
5. **Items.** These vary throughout the site and can be many different things, depending on what part of the site you are currently using. For example, if you are in the User screen, the items show the users. If you are on the Module screen, this shows the modules. If you are in the Article Manager, this shows the articles, as in the figure below:

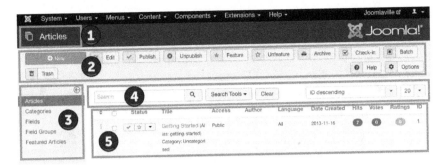

Let's take a look at another example. Visit Joomla's Menus screen by clicking on "Menus" and then "All Menu Items", as in the image below:

You see a screen like the one below. The same 5 features that we saw in the Article screen are available here in the All Menu Items screen also:

1. Page title.
2. Action buttons.
3. Submenu.
4. Search.
5. Items.

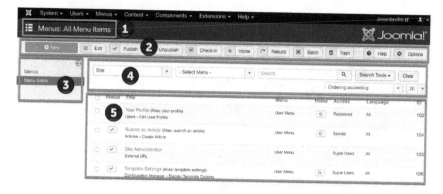

Go ahead and click on some other links, especially those under Components and Extensions. You see the same layout almost everywhere you go. Hopefully, this makes your life easier in several ways:

- **Not sure where you are?** Look at the page title.

- **Can't find an item?** Just use the search box or the filters.

- **Need to add, modify or create an item?** Look for all the action buttons.

### Individual Page Layouts

It's not only the pages from the dropdown menu that nearly always look the same. When you click through to an individual page, the layout is also consistent.

Let's go back to Joomla's Article screen by clicking on "Content", then "Article" and then click on "Getting Started", as in the figure below:

You now see Joomla's main content creation screen. There are four key features, as shown in the image below:

1. **Page title.** This tells you where you are in your administrator area.
2. **Action buttons.** These buttons allow you to modify any of the items you see.
3. **Content.** This is why you're visiting this part of the site. For example, if you're in an article, this will be the main article text.
4. **Options.** These are the most important settings that you can change.

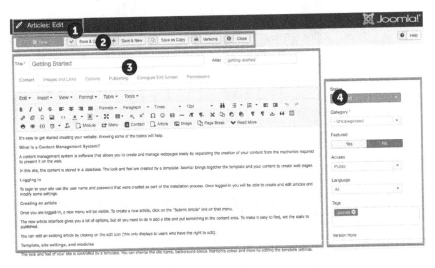

Let's take a look at one more example:

- Click "Save & Close" in the action buttons, as in the image below:

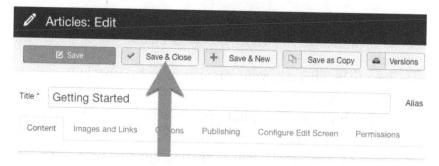

- Click on "Extensions", then "Modules", as in the image below:

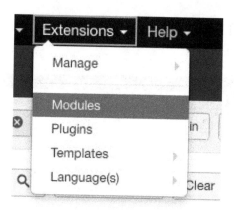

- Click on the "Latest Articles" link, as shown below:

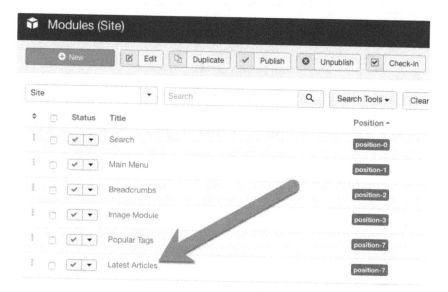

You now see a screen like the one in the image below. The same four features that we saw in the Article editing screen are available here also:

1. **Page title.**
2. **Action buttons.**
3. **Content.**
4. **Options.**

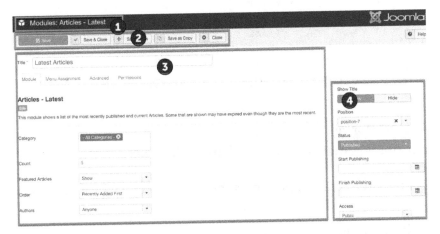

Joomla is easy to use because it's consistent:

- **Not sure where you are?** Look at the title.

- **Need to modify this page?** Look for all the action buttons in the top-left corner.

- **Need to edit the important parts of the page?** Look at the options on the right-hand side.

Now that we've seen the administrator area in more detail, let's look at the visitor area. To access the visitor area, click the link in the top-right of your screen, as shown in the image below:

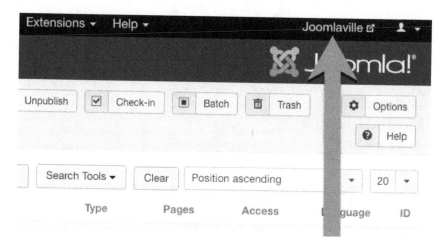

## UNDERSTANDING THE VISITOR AREA OF YOUR JOOMLA SITE

This visitor area is why you build your site. It shows all the information that you want to share with people.

Your visitor area should look similar to the screen below:

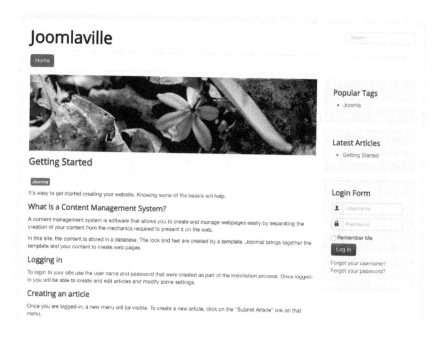

There is already one article on your site, called "Getting

Started". There are also three boxes on the right-hand side. Joomla calls these "modules":

- Popular Tags
- Latest Articles
- Login Form

Earlier in this chapter, we saw that the administrator area is where you change your site. Now that we've seen the visitor area as well, we'll see how the two areas work together. Let's go and actually make our first changes.

To make changes, we need to go back to the administrator area. To do this, add /administrator to your site's URL or click on your bookmark for the Joomla administrator area.

## MAKING YOUR FIRST JOOMLA SITE CHANGES

Now that you know a little about navigating through the Joomla administrator area, let's see how easy it is to make some changes to your site.

Let's modify the Getting Started article so it reflects the fact that our site is about Joomlaville.

- Click on "Content", then "Articles".
- Click on "Getting Started". You'll now see a screen like the image below, exactly as we saw earlier in the chapter.
- Change "Getting Started" in the title to "About Joomlaville".
- Change "getting-started" in the Alias box to "about-joomlaville". This is a part of the URL of this article.

- Now select all the text in the article and delete it. Your screen will look like the image below:

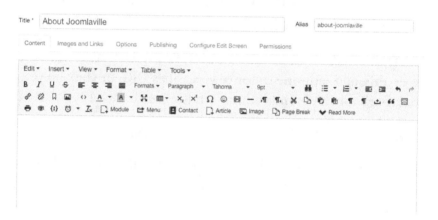

- You can either type your own text, or https://ostraining.com/ books/j3e/chapter4/ has some text that you can use for this article. You can copy and paste the text from that site into your new article.

It's worth pointing out here that copying and pasting text will not always be as easy as it is here. Some programs such as Microsoft Word are notorious for creating a lot of bad formatting with their articles. If you do have copy-and-paste problems, start by copying from the article and pasting into a text editor like WordPad or Notepad. That clears away the formatting. You can then copy the code out of the editor and paste into Joomla.

- Click "Save & Close" in the action buttons area.
- Click on the "Joomlaville" link, in the top-right corner. This will take you to the visitor area.
- You'll now see your updated article, as in the figure below:

Congratulations! You've just updated your first Joomla content.

Let's take this one step further and create some new content:

- Go to the administrator area of your site.
- Click on "Content" then "Articles".
- Click on the green "New" button, as shown below:

We are going to enter 3 things for our first new article. These 3 items are marked in the image below:

1. **Title.** Enter "Our New Joomlaville Website".
2. **Text.** Enter some text in the main body.
3. **Category**. Type "News". This category doesn't exist, however, if you enter a new category name, Joomla will automatically create it for you.

- Click "Save & Close".
- Click on the Joomlaville link, in the top-right corner.
- Click "Our New Joomlaville Website" in the "Latest Articles" module, as shown below:

- You'll now see your article, as in the image below:

Congratulations! You've just updated your first Joomla content!

You used the administrator area of your site to update the visitor area. You can now see how the two areas of your site are connected.

You're ready for the next steps in building your first Joomla site.

WHAT'S NEXT?

In this chapter, we saw how to modify and add new articles.

In the next chapter, we're going to explore articles in more depth. Your content is the most important thing on your site, so we'll show you how to add it, organize it and make it look great.

Turn the page, and let's get started.

# CHAPTER 5.

## JOOMLA CONTENT EXPLAINED

---

This chapter explains the easiest and fastest way to add content to a Joomla site. If you follow this workflow, it will make your Joomla life very easy.

The workflow for adding Joomla content is simple:

- **Step 1: Categorize.** Create organization for your articles.
- **Step 2: Add.** Write your articles.
- **Step 3: Show.** Make menu links so that people can click on them and see your articles.

I like to call this the *CASh* workflow. CASh is short for Categorize, Add, Show. It does take a little bit of practice to follow the workflow correctly. But once you run through the workflow a few times, it should become easy to add content to your Joomla site.

After reading this chapter, you'll be able to do the following:

- Organize your Joomla content into categories
- Add new content to Joomla
- Show your content in various ways, including a full page, a blog with intro text, or a long list of articles.

## STEP 1: CATEGORIZE

The first step in the Joomla content workflow is to categorize our content. We need to make sure that our information can be usefully organized.

Let's think about the Joomlaville project we started in the previous chapters. What do we need to include on the website for our visitors? To plan our site's organization, grab a piece of paper and a pen and brainstorm.

Go ahead and write down all the articles you want on your site. For this small site, your list might look something like the list I have below:

- Climate
- Location
- History
- Museum
- Zoo
- Aquarium
- Trains
- Buses
- Airport

Now that we know what information we want to have on our site, let's organize it.

Joomla uses categories to organize articles. Let's create one category for each group of related articles and name it appropriately, as seen below:

**Information**

- Climate

- Location
- History

**Attractions**

- Museum
- Zoo
- Aquarium

**Transport**

- Trains
- Buses
- Airport

Here are those categories in visual form:

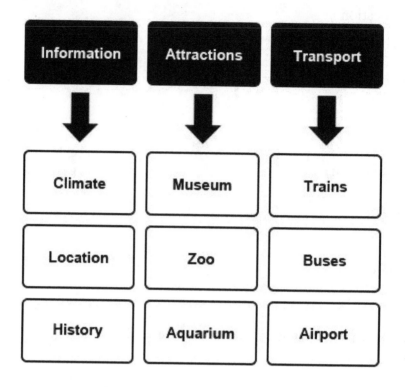

Things can get much more advanced, but this is a nice straightforward example to get us started.

Now that we've finished our plan, we are ready to start implementing that plan in Joomla. We use the CASh workflow to create the first category called *Information* and the three articles inside called *Climate, Location,* and *History.* Here's the process we use:

- **Step 1**: Categorize. Create the Information category.
- **Step 2**: Add. Write your three articles.
- **Step 3**: Show. Make menu links so that people can click through and see your articles.

Ready? Let's get started and use Joomla's CASh workflow for the first time:

- Go to your administrator area, click on "Content" and then click on "Categories". You'll see a page like the one in the figure below:

You can see that Uncategorised and News are already options. The Uncategorised category is used for articles that really don't fit in any other category. It's most commonly used for small sites with only five or six articles. With so few articles, you wouldn't really need to divide them into categories. However, we're going to have at least a dozen articles, so we need to create more categories.

- Click the green "New" button.
- Title: **Information**.
- Description: **This category contains information about Joomlaville.**

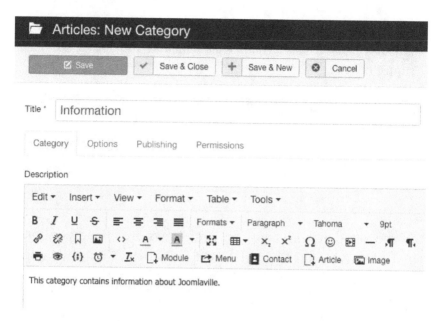

- Click "Save & Close". You should see that your category has been added, as seen below. You'll see a message which says, "Category saved".

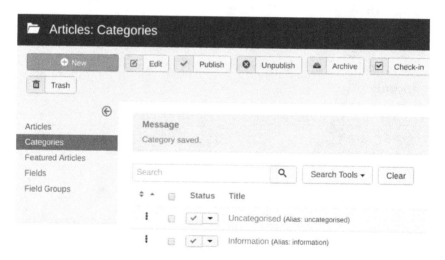

Now that we have a category to organize our articles, let's go and write those articles.

## STEP 2: ADD

To start writing, let's go and create a new article:

- Click "Content", then"Articles", and then "Add New Article".

The articles have a lot of options, but there are only three fields you must fill in:

1. Title
2. Content
3. Category

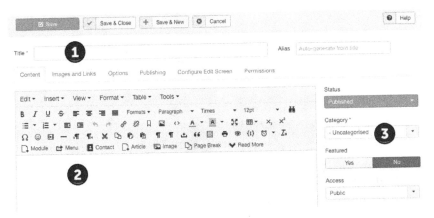

Let's fill in those three fields from top to bottom:

- Title: **Climate**

Using "Climate" matches the first article in our plan. When you save the article, the Title is automatically copied into the Alias field. This Alias field forms part of the article URL, so our Climate article will have a URL that contains "climate". You can find out more about how Joomla creates URLs in the chapter called "Joomla Site Management Explained".

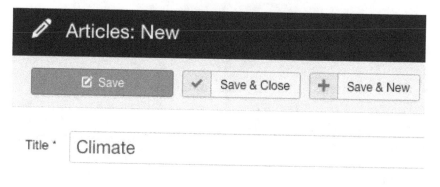

Title * Climate

- Category: **Information**

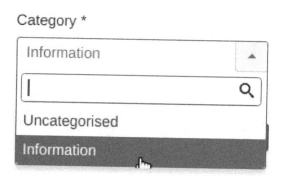

- Finally, write the article. There is some sample text at https://ostraining.com/books/j3e/chapter5/ that you can use for this article.

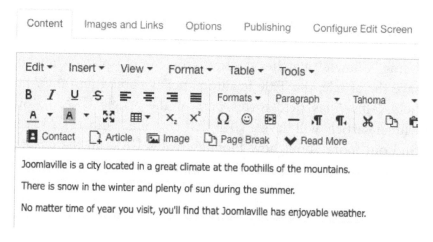

Joomlaville is a city located in a great climate at the foothills of the mountains.

There is snow in the winter and plenty of sun during the summer.

No matter time of year you visit, you'll find that Joomlaville has enjoyable weather.

- Click "Save & Close".

- If you visit the front of your site and click "Climate" in the "Latest Articles" module, your article will look like the image below:

Let's go ahead and repeat that process again. Here are the details for our second article in the Information category:

1. Title: **Location**
2. Category: **Information**
3. Article Text: Describe where the city is. There is some sample text at https://ostraining.com/books/j3e/ chapter5/ to help you out.

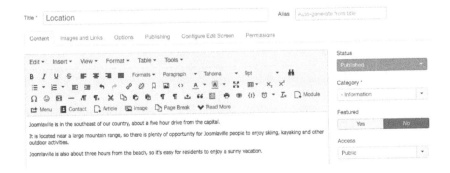

Let's do that one more time to finish our Information category with the third article. Here are the details we use:

1.  Title: **History**
2.  Category: **Information**
3.  Article Text: Use the sample text at https://ostraining.com/books/j3e/chapter5/.

Wonderful! We now have one new category on our site called Information, and it contains three new articles: Climate, Location, and History.

There's only one thing left to do.

Go and visit the front of your site. Have a look at your site and the image shown below. What's missing?

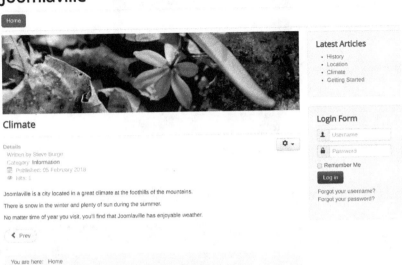

There's no easy way to see your new "Information" articles.

Yes, there's the "Latest Articles" module, but that will soon be updated with new articles.

Our solution will be to make new menu links so visitors can see our articles.

We've done two steps of our Joomla CASh workflow: Categorize and Add. The third and final step is Show.

## STEP 3: SHOW

We need to show people our articles. We do that by making menu links to the articles:

- In the administrator drop-down menu, click on "Menus" then "Main Menu".

You currently only have a single menu link to Home:

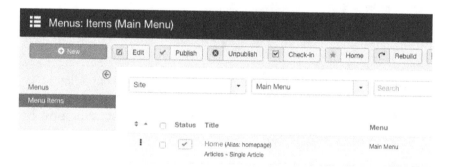

We're going to add a new link to the Information articles we created earlier.

- Click "New" in the top-left corner.
- You will now see a screen like the image below. Whenever you create a menu link to any part of your site, you'll always see this same screen.

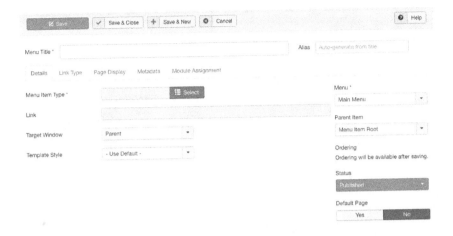

- Click on the blue "Select" button. This will allow you to decide which part of the site to link to.

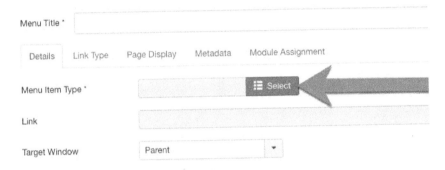

- You'll see a pop-up screen with all sorts of different options. Each one allows you to link to a different part of your Joomla site. You could link to a contact form, a search box, a registration form, or many other features. We want to link to one of the articles we created earlier, so click "Articles" and choose "Category Blog", as shown below:

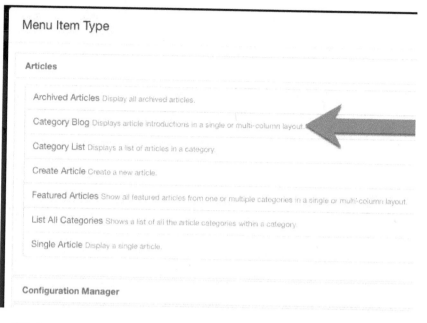

Menu Item Type

**Articles**

Archived Articles Display all archived articles.

Category Blog Displays article introductions in a single or multi-column layout.

Category List Displays a list of articles in a category.

Create Article Create a new article.

Featured Articles Show all featured articles from one or multiple categories in a single or multi-column layout.

List All Categories Shows a list of all the article categories within a category.

Single Article Display a single article.

**Configuration Manager**

- We have just chosen to link to a category. Now let's choose *which* category. Click on the "Select" button, as in the image below:

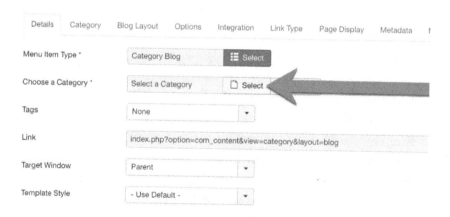

| Details | Category | Blog Layout | Options | Integration | Link Type | Page Display | Metadata |
|---|---|---|---|---|---|---|---|

Menu Item Type *      Category Blog        ▤ Select

Choose a Category *    Select a Category      ☐ Select

Tags                  None              ▾

Link                  index.php?option=com_content&view=category&layout=blog

Target Window         Parent            ▾

Template Style        - Use Default -   ▾

- You'll see another pop-up box. Click on the "Information" link".

Select or Change Category

| Status | Title | | Access | Language |
|--------|-------|---|--------|----------|
| ✓ | Uncategorised | | Public | All |
| ✓ | Information | | Public | All |

- Enter "Information" in the Menu Title field, as shown below:

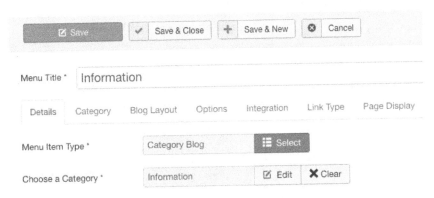

Menu Title * Information

Details | Category | Blog Layout | Options | Integration | Link Type | Page Display

Menu Item Type * — Category Blog — Select

Choose a Category * — Information — Edit — Clear

- Click "Save & Close" to complete the creation of your menu link.
- Visit the front of your site, and you'll see your new Information link on the Main Menu:

Joomlaville

Home | Information

- Click on the Information link, and you'll see your new articles published on your site:

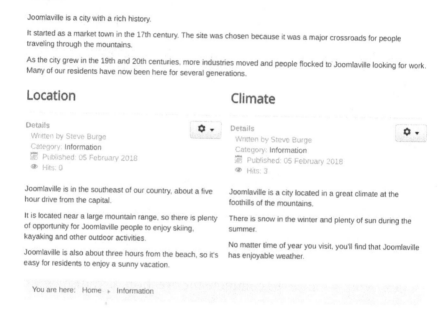

## History

Details
Written by Steve Burge
Category: Information
Published: 05 February 2018
Hits: 0

Joomlaville is a city with a rich history.

It started as a market town in the 17th century. The site was chosen because it was a major crossroads for people traveling through the mountains.

As the city grew in the 19th and 20th centuries, more industries moved and people flocked to Joomlaville looking for work. Many of our residents have now been here for several generations.

## Location

Details
Written by Steve Burge
Category: Information
Published: 05 February 2018
Hits: 0

Joomlaville is in the southeast of our country, about a five hour drive from the capital.

It is located near a large mountain range, so there is plenty of opportunity for Joomlaville people to enjoy skiing, kayaking and other outdoor activities.

Joomlaville is also about three hours from the beach, so it's easy for residents to enjoy a sunny vacation.

## Climate

Details
Written by Steve Burge
Category: Information
Published: 05 February 2018
Hits: 3

Joomlaville is a city located in a great climate at the foothills of the mountains.

There is snow in the winter and plenty of sun during the summer.

No matter time of year you visit, you'll find that Joomlaville has enjoyable weather.

You are here: Home › Information

That's it. You've done it! Both you and your visitors can now see your new articles.

THE JOOMLA CASH WORKFLOW: WHY DO IT THIS WAY?

- Step 1: Categorize
- Step 2: Add
- Step 3: Show

Those are three steps for adding content to a Joomla site.

However, why do it this way? Why not make our menu links first? Why not write our articles first? Why bother making links at all?

Here are answers to some of the questions you might have at the moment:

- **Why not make our menu links first?** Because we wouldn't have anything to link to. We wouldn't have any articles to show.

- **Why create our categories first?** Imagine you build a big Joomla site. You might be planning 50, 500, or even 5,000 articles. I've seen Joomla sites with more than 100,000 articles. How would you organize that many articles? Categories allow us to organize all our articles.

- **Why bother making menu links?** Remember when we first added our articles but couldn't see them on our site? Menu links are what allow people to see our articles. If people can't click through to the articles, they can't see them.

We regularly meet Joomla students who have tried to teach themselves and got stuck. Most of the time it's because they didn't know about this workflow:

- Some of them tried to make their menu links first and wondered why they had so few choices.

- Some people wrote all their articles first and then ended up with a big mess of unorganized articles.

- Some people added their categories and articles and then stopped. They looked at their site and got frustrated because they couldn't see what they'd written.

Follow the workflow, and creating your Joomla content will be easy. Here it is one more time:

- **Step 1: Categorize.** Create categories so that you can organize your articles.

- **Step 2: Add.** Write your articles.

- **Step 3: Show.** Make menu links so that people can click through and see your articles.

Now that we've learned the Joomla CASh workflow, let's practice it.

PRACTICING THE CASH WORKFLOW

Think back to the categories and pages we planned earlier:

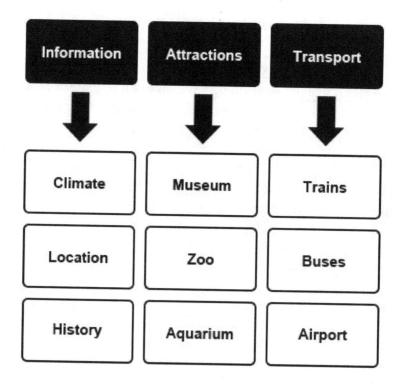

We've done that first category: Information. Here's what we're going to do. We're going to give you a full step-by-step guide to creating the Attractions category, articles, and menu links. Then we're going to let you try and do the Transport category by yourself. I've provided sample text for all of them at https://ostraining.com/books/j3e/chapter5/.

## Step 1: Categorize

- Go to "Content", "Categories", then "Add New Category".

- Enter **Attractions** in the Title field and click "Save & Close". Check that your Category list looks like the image below.

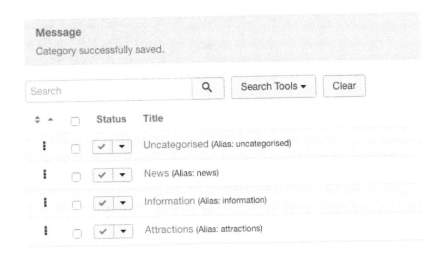

## Step 2: Add

- Go to "Content", "Articles", then "Add New Article".

- Title: **Museum**

- Category: **Attractions**

- Copy and paste the text from https://ostraining.com/books/j3e/chapter5/.

- Click "Save & Close".

Repeat this process with the Zoo and Aquarium articles. Check that your Article screen looks like the image below:

| ⇕ | ☐ | Status | Title |
|---|---|--------|-------|
| ⦙ | ☐ | ✔ ☆ ▾ | About Joomlaville (Alias: about-joomlaville)<br>Category: Uncategorised |
| ⦙ | ☐ | ✔ ☆ ▾ | Our New Joomlaville Website (Alias: our-new-joomlaville-website)<br>Category: News |
| ⦙ | ☐ | ✔ ☆ ▾ | Climate (Alias: climate)<br>Category: Information |
| ⦙ | ☐ | ✔ ☆ ▾ | Location (Alias: location)<br>Category: Information |
| ⦙ | ☐ | ✔ ☆ ▾ | History (Alias: history)<br>Category: Information |
| ⦙ | ☐ | ✔ ☆ ▾ | Museum (Alias: museum)<br>Category: Attractions |
| ⦙ | ☐ | ✔ ☆ ▾ | Zoo (Alias: zoo)<br>Category: Attractions |
| ⦙ | ☐ | ✔ ☆ ▾ | Aquarium (Alias: aquarium)<br>Category: Attractions |

## Step 3: Show

- Go to "Menus", "Main Menu", then "Add New Menu Item".
- Menu Title: **Attractions**
- Click "Select" next to Menu Item Type.
- Click on "Articles" in the pop-up, and choose "Category Blog".
- Click "Select" next to Choose a Category, and then click on"Attractions".

- Click "Save & Close".
- Check that your Menu screen looks like the figure below.

- Visit the front of your site and make sure your new menu link is working:

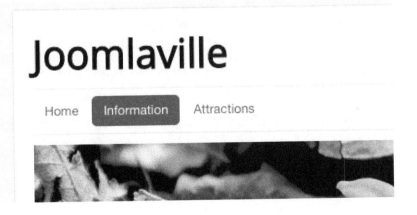

- Click on the "Attractions" link, and you will see the articles you've written, as shown in the image below:

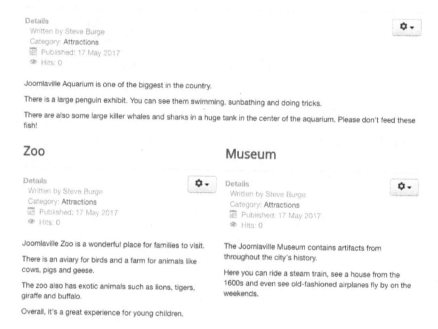

### Aquarium

Details
Written by Steve Burge
Category: Attractions
Published: 17 May 2017
Hits: 0

Joomlaville Aquarium is one of the biggest in the country.

There is a large penguin exhibit. You can see them swimming, sunbathing and doing tricks.

There are also some large killer whales and sharks in a huge tank in the center of the aquarium. Please don't feed these fish!

### Zoo

Details
Written by Steve Burge
Category: Attractions
Published: 17 May 2017
Hits: 0

Joomlaville Zoo is a wonderful place for families to visit.

There is an aviary for birds and a farm for animals like cows, pigs and geese.

The zoo also has exotic animals such as lions, tigers, giraffe and buffalo.

Overall, it's a great experience for young children.

### Museum

Details
Written by Steve Burge
Category: Attractions
Published: 17 May 2017
Hits: 0

The Joomlaville Museum contains artifacts from throughout the city's history.

Here you can ride a steam train, see a house from the 1600s and even see old-fashioned airplanes fly by on the weekends.

Congratulations! Hopefully, that wasn't too bad! If you're ready, let's see if you can do that again but without step-by-step directions:

- Your task is to create the Transport categories, articles, and menu link.

- Sample text for all 3 articles is available at https://ostraining.com/books/j3e/chapter5/.

- If you get stuck, don't worry. Full instructions are also available at https://ostraining.com/books/j3e/chapter5/.

- Afterwards, your link and articles should look like the image below:

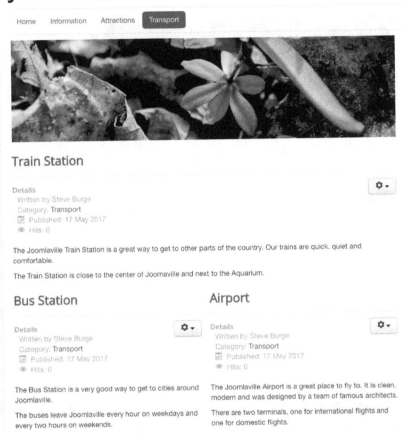

If we take a step back and look at your whole site, it should look like the screen below:

You've done an excellent job to get this far, and by understanding the CASh workflow, you've unlocked the key to building a Joomla site.

If you put this chapter down and don't remember anything but Joomla's CASh workflow, you'll be in good shape. Write it down, print it on a T-shirt, sing it in the shower, tattoo it on your arm, or do whatever else you need to do to remember it. This is how you add content to your Joomla site:

- **Step 1: Categorize.** Create categories so that you can organize your articles.

- **Step 2: Add.** Write your articles.

- **Step 3: Show.** Make menu links so that people can click through and see your articles.

WHAT'S NEXT?

We now know how to organize, create, and show our articles.

That's great, but currently, those articles aren't very interesting. The articles are just plain text. There's no formatting, no images, and no links to other pages. That's the problem we're going to solve in the next chapter, "Joomla Content Editing Explained".

Turn the page, and we show you how to create articles with formatting, images, links, and more.

# CHAPTER 6.

## JOOMLA CONTENT EDITING EXPLAINED

---

We currently have about a dozen articles on our site.

It's now time to make those articles more interesting. In this chapter, we focus on making your articles more exciting.

Specifically, we will work on formatting the text, adding images and links, and choosing the best options for your articles.

After reading this chapter, you'll be able to do the following:

- Format the text of your Joomla articles
- Add images to your content
- Add links between different articles and to other sites
- Choose the best publishing, article, and metadata options for your articles

### FORMATTING YOUR TEXT

In the previous chapters, we added articles to our site. However, we only wrote in a plain text. We didn't use any bold text, italics, bullet points, or indeed any type of formatting.

Fortunately, formatting text is easy in Joomla. If you can do formatting in your e-mail or in Microsoft Word, you can do it in Joomla.

Let's start by editing our "About Joomlaville" article:

- Go to "Content", then "Articles", and then "About Joomlaville". Your article should look like the screen shown in the image below.

Your formatting options are all above the text. Let's take a closer look at them. The buttons are shown in the image below, and many will be familiar if you've done any word processing before. The process for using the editor is simple: Select text you want to format and then click the formatting button.

The Joomla formatting buttons work in the same way as e-mail and Microsoft Word buttons. Let's show you how to use them:

- Using your cursor, select the first text in the article: "Thank you for visiting our site for the city of Joomlaville."

- Choose the **B** button in the top-left of the formatting options. This is the button to make your text bold. As you're doing this, your screen looks like the figure below:

When you're finished, your text will be in bold, as shown in the image below:

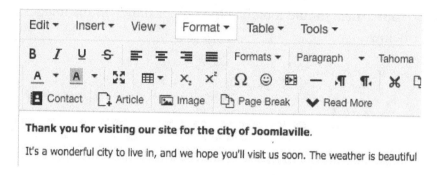

Let's repeat that process but with the italics option. Here's how we do it:

- Start by selecting the words "wonderful city".

- Click on the *I* button in the top-left of the formatting options. This is the button to make your text italic. As you're doing this, your screen looks like the image below:

When you're finished, your text will be in italics, as in the image below:

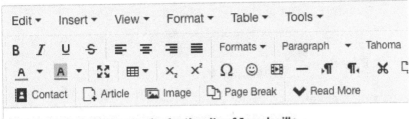

Next up is the option to align your text. You can choose from left, center, right and justify alignments. As before, select the text you want to align and click the appropriate button. If you choose the Justify alignment, your text will be forced to spread out so that it touches both the left and the right-hand side of the article.

The image below shows right-aligned text. You can remove any alignment options by selecting the text and clicking the left alignment button.

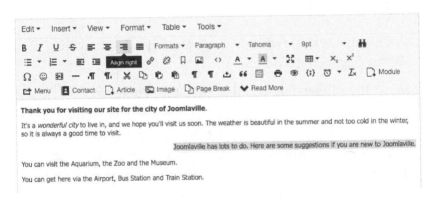

Further along the editing row is a series of dropdowns: Format, Paragraph, Tahoma, and 9pt. These are formatting features which allow you to select different styles for your text:

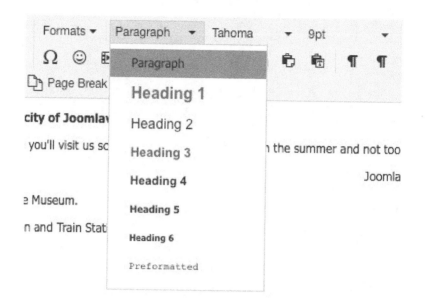

For example, in the second half of the Welcome to Joomlaville article, we have suggestions for site visitors. We can put a subheading in there to break up the text and make it easier to read. Here's how we do it:

- Use normal text to write your subheading: "Joomlaville Visitor Suggestions".

- Select the subheading text and click the "Paragraph" dropdown. Choose "Heading 3". We choose Heading 3 here because Heading 1 and Heading 2 are normally associated with the article title or the other very important headings on the page.

- You should now see "Joomlaville Visitor Suggestions" in slightly larger, blue text:

**Thank you for visiting our site for the city of Joomlaville.**

It's a *wonderful city* to live in, and we hope you'll visit us soon. The weather is beautiful

**Joomlaville Visitor Suggestions**

Joomlaville has lots to do. Here are some suggestions if you are new to Joomlaville.

You can visit the Aquarium, the Zoo and the Museum.

You can get here via the Airport, Bus Station and Train Station.

There are far more options in the editor than we can cover in this book, but we can show you some useful extra features. One feature you are likely to use is bullet points. You can make either an unordered list with bullet points or an ordered list with numbers. Here's how to create a bulleted list:

- Put your cursor after the word "visit" in the sentence "You can visit the Aquarium, the Zoo and the Museum."

- Hit Enter or Return to move the attractions onto a new line.

- Make sure your cursor is in front of "the Aquarium" and click the unordered list button.

- Make sure your cursor is in front of "the Zoo" and click Return or Enter.

- Make sure your cursor is in front of "the Museum" and click Return or Enter.

You can now tidy up the punctuation, removing commas and adding a semicolon. Your screen should look like the figure below:

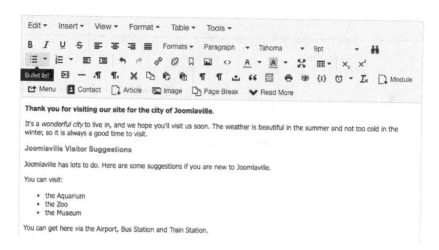

**Thank you for visiting our site for the city of Joomlaville.**

It's a *wonderful city* to live in, and we hope you'll visit us soon. The weather is beautiful in the summer and not too cold in the winter, so it is always a good time to visit.

**Joomlaville Visitor Suggestions**

Joomlaville has lots to do. Here are some suggestions if you are new to Joomlaville.

You can visit:

- the Aquarium
- the Zoo
- the Museum

You can get here via the Airport, Bus Station and Train Station.

## What if I Made a Mistake?

There's no need to worry if you made a mistake while working on your article. To undo a mistake, click on the back arrow, which is shown below. Clicking this will undo the last change you made. The Undo button is highlighted in the image below. Next to the Undo button is a Redo button, so you can reapply any changes that you have undone.

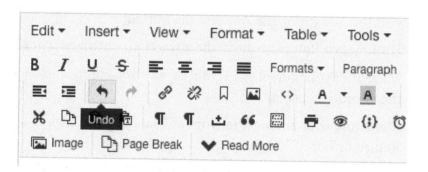

Now, let's see what our article looks like live on the site:

- Click the "Save" button.
- Click the "Joomlaville" link in the top-right corner.
- Your article will look similar to the image below:

## About Joomlaville

**Thank you for visiting our site for the city of Joomlaville.**

It's a *wonderful city* to live in, and we hope you'll visit us soon. The weather is beautiful in the summer and not too cold in the winter, so it is always a good time to visit.

### Joomlaville Visitor Suggestions

Joomlaville has lots to do. Here are some suggestions if you are new to Joomlaville.

You can visit:

- the Aquarium
- the Zoo
- the Museum

You can get here via the Airport, Bus Station and Train Station.

We formatted our text, but the article still looks a little plain. Let's add some images to our Joomlaville articles and show our visitors what Joomlaville looks like.

## ADDING IMAGES TO YOUR CONTENT

Remember the CASh workflow we used in Chapter 5, "Joomla Content Explained" to add content?

1. Categorize
2. Add
3. Show

We use exactly the same CASh workflow for adding images.

### Categorize Images

- Go to "Content" and then "Media".
- When you're in the Media area, you see a screen like the one below. It contains all the images you uploaded to your site. At the moment, all you should see are a few sample images:

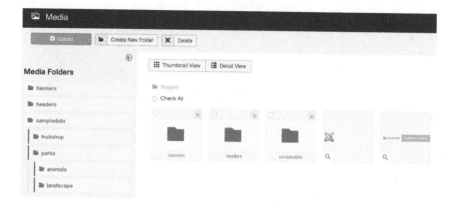

As with articles, we start by organizing our images. We created categories to organize our articles, and we're going to create folders to organize our images. If we build a large site, it's going to be much easier to find a particular image if they are all logically organized. One logical approach is to create an image folder for each of our article categories. For our example, that means all the images we use in our Attractions articles go into an image folder of the same name. Here's how we create that folder:

- Click the "Create New Folder" button.

- A small box will slide down. Enter the word "attractions" into this box.

- Click "Create Folder".

- Repeat the process for our other categories: information, transport, news and uncategorized. When you're finished, your screen should look like the one below:

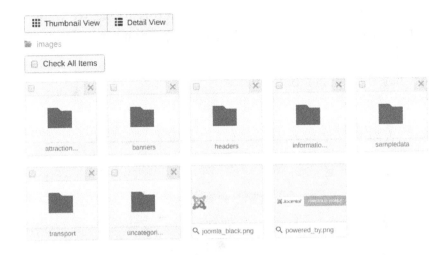

You can add your images via the Media Manager using the Upload button on this screen. However, it's easier to upload your image files when you're writing your articles.

### Add Images

Let's start by placing an image in our About Joomlaville article:

- Go to "Content", then "Articles", and then "About Joomlaville".
- Go to https://ostraining.com/books/j3e/chapter6/, and you see an image called "Town Hall".
- Download the Town Hall image to your desktop. To do this, click the Download link under the image. Some computers automatically download image files to your desktop. On other computers, you see the image and need to right-click on it and use the "Save Image As" option to download it to your desktop. Before you move on, check to make sure that the image has actually been downloaded to your computer.

Now we can upload and add that image to our article. Here's how we do it:

- Select the place where you want to insert the image. Do this by putting your cursor into the text. In this article, we want the image at the top of the article, so I put the cursor before "Thank you".

- Click the "Image" button:

- You'll now see a pop-up window like the one in the image below. This will show all of the files and folders that we saw on the Media screen:

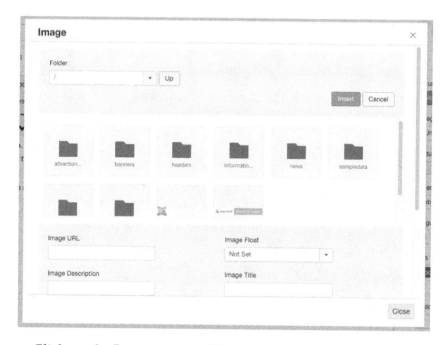

- Click on the "uncategorized" folder, because that's where we want to upload the image. You'll see a message saying "No Images Found", as in the image below:

- Scroll down until you see a "Choose Files" button, as shown in the screen below:

- Choose the image that you downloaded. You'll see that Joomla shows the name of the image, which is townhall.jpg. Click the "Start Upload" button.
- You'll now see that the Town Hall image has been successfully uploaded:

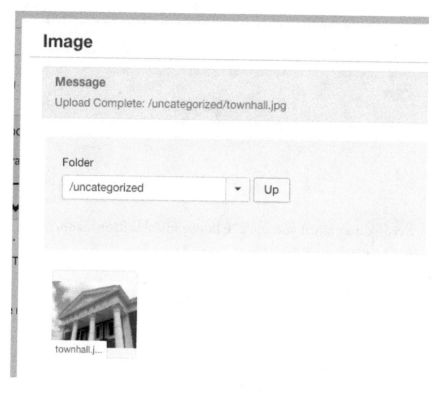

## Show Images

Now that our images have been uploaded to our Joomla site, we can start inserting them in our article. Here's how we do it:

- Click on the townhall.jpg image so that it is selected, with a check in the top-right corner.
- Click "Insert".

The image now appears on the left of the article:

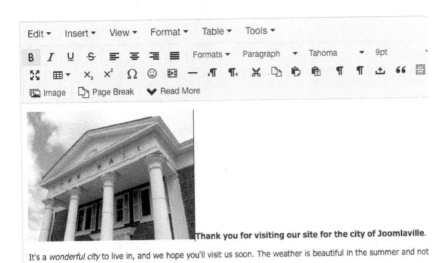

What we now need to do is move the image to the right of the screen:

- Select the image so that the corners are highlighted.
- Click the "align right" button in the toolbar again:

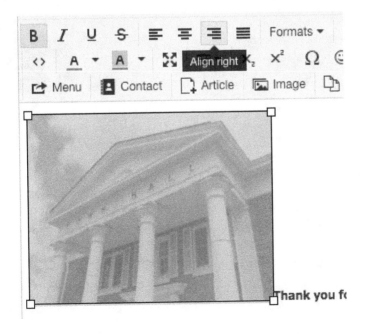

- You should now see the image on the right of your article, with the text wrapped around:

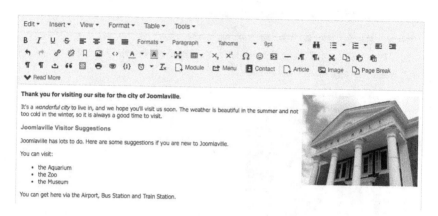

- Click "Save" and then visit the front of your site so you can see how your new image looks to visitors. It should look like the image below:

## About Joomlaville

**Thank you for visiting our site for the city of Joomlaville.**

It's a *wonderful city* to live in, and we hope you'll visit us soon. The weather is beautiful in the summer and not too cold in the winter, so it is always a good time to visit.

### Joomlaville Visitor Suggestions

Joomlaville has lots to do. Here are some suggestions if you are new to Joomlaville.

You can visit:

- the Aquarium
- the Zoo
- the Museum

You can get here via the Airport, Bus Station and Train Station.

## What If I Made a Mistake?

If you don't like the size of the image or how it's placed in your article, you have several ways to fix the mistake.

You can manually resize images inside your article. Click the image inside your article, and you see a small square on each corner and edge of the image. You can click on these squares and drag them to resize the image, as shown in the figure below:

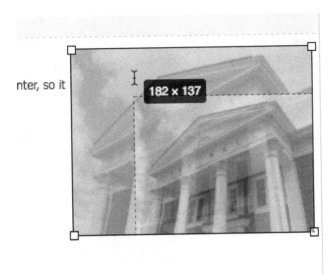

You can also change the image options. Click the image inside your article, and the small picture button becomes highlighted, as shown below:

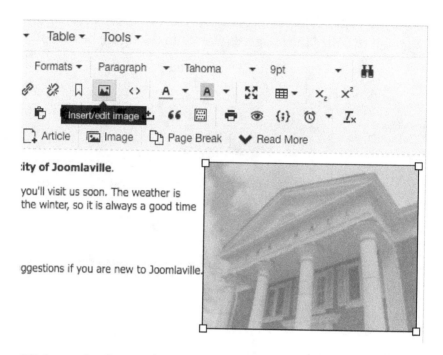

Click on the "Insert/edit image" button, and you see a pop-up screen where you can edit the image settings. You can change the image's width and height here:

## Insert/edit image ✕

General    Advanced

| | |
|---|---|
| Source | images/uncategorized/townhall.jpg |
| Image description | |
| Image Title | |
| Dimensions | 246 x 185 ✔ Constrain proportions |

Ok    Cancel

So we now have a formatted article with images. However, there are still many more useful things we can do with our content.

To take just one example, we have sentences like this on our site's home page: "You can visit the Aquarium, the Zoo and the Museum."

However, how do visitors find the information pages for the Aquarium, Zoo or Museum? They need a link to those pages, and that's what we're going to do next.

## ADDING LINKS TO YOUR CONTENT

Now that we know how to add images, let's see how to add links to our Joomla articles.

### Internal Links

Let's start by editing the article we've been using throughout this chapter: "About Joomlaville." The process for adding links to text is the same as for adding formatting: Select and then click.

- Select the text that you want to be linked. In this example, let's choose the word "Aquarium".
- Click the "Article" button in the editor, as in the image below:

- You see a pop-up window with a list of all your articles. Find the Aquarium article that you want to link to and click on the article title, like shown on the screen below:

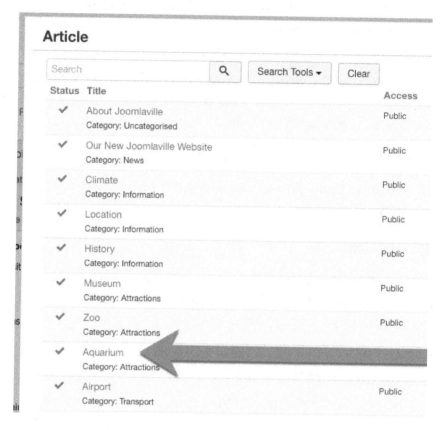

That's it. There will now be a link to the article you chose. Two things to note:

- If the article title is different from the text you selected, the article title will be used. If you don't want to use the article title, you can put your cursor on the text and edit it.
- These links won't work in the Article Editor, but they will when you go to the visitors' area of your site.

Now, see if you can add more links to our About Joomlaville articles. Go ahead and add links from these words to the appropriate articles: Zoo, Museum, Airport, Bus Station, and Train Station. Your article will look like the image below:

## External Links

For linking to other Web sites, we use a different button. In this article, we also need a good reason to link to an external site, so let's set that up first:

- Add a new line of text at the bottom of the article: **Who Lives in Joomlaville?**
- Select the text: Who Lives in Joomlaville?
- Click the "Formats" button and choose Header 3.
- Write a short paragraph under the subheading: "Joomlaville is full of people who love Joomla! Find out more at the official Joomla website."

**Joomlaville Visitor Suggestions**

Joomlaville has lots to do. Here are some suggestions if you are new to Joomlaville.

You can visit:

- the Aquarium
- the Zoo
- the Museum

You can get here via the Airport, Bus Station and Train Station.

**Who Lives in Joomlaville?**

Joomlaville is full of people who love Joomla! Find out more at the official Joomla website.

- Select "the official Joomla website" in the text.
- Click the link icon in the editor area, as shown in the figure below:

| **our site for the city of Joomlaville**.

ve in, and we hope you'll visit us soon. The weather is
and not too cold in the winter, so it is always a good

**iggestions**

). Here are some suggestions if you are new to

Airport, Bus Station and Train Station.

ville?

)le who love Joomla! Find out more at the official Joomla website.

- You see a pop-up screen like the one shown below. Enter **http://joomla.org** into the Url field. The text in the Title field is what visitors will see and click on to use the link. Change the "Target" field to "New window" if you want the link to open a new window in the visitor's browser. Click OK to complete the link:

- You can now click "Save & Close" and visit the front of your site to see your updated About Joomlaville article. It should look like the image below:

### About Joomlaville

**Thank you for visiting our site for the city of Joomlaville.**

It's a *wonderful city* to live in, and we hope you'll visit us soon. The weather is beautiful in the summer and not too cold in the winter, so it is always a good time to visit.

### Joomlaville Visitor Suggestions

Joomlaville has lots to do. Here are some suggestions if you are new to Joomlaville.

You can visit:

- the Aquarium
- the Zoo
- the Museum

You can get here via the Airport, Bus Station and Train Station.

### Who Lives in Joomlaville?

Joomlaville is full of people who love Joomla! Find out more at the official Joomla website.

## What If I Made a Mistake?

The process for removing an incorrect link is similar to the process we've been using so far: Select and click.

- Select the text you want to remove the link from.

- Click the small "Remove link" icon in the editor area. As you're doing this, your screen looks like the image below:

## VERSIONS OF YOUR ARTICLES

During this chapter, we've had several sections called "What if I Made a Mistake?" We saw several ways to roll back from a change that you made.

Now we're going to see how to roll back from changes for your whole article, even if you made them months ago:

- Inside your About Joomlaville article, click the "Versions" button at the top of the screen:

You'll now see a pop-up. Every time you click "Save" for an article, Joomla will store a copy of the article. In the image below, Joomla has saved many versions of this article. The version marked with the gold star is the current version.

- To see the differences between two versions, check the boxes next to them and click the "Compare" button.

Joomla shows you both versions of the article, side-by-side. On the right-hand side, there's also a column showing the changes. Although you may not be able to see the colors in the image below, additions are marked in green and deletions are marked in red. Unfortunately, this Versions system doesn't display images:

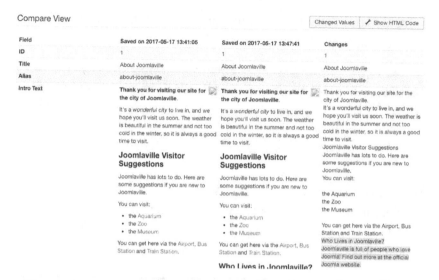

- If you do decide that you want to restore the previous version of an article, check the box next to it and click the Restore button, as shown in the figure below:

## WHAT'S NEXT?

We've added great articles to our site, but we can do better. At the moment, we've only used a single text area.

Joomla allows us to add more than just text. We can also add fields that are full of different types of information.

Turn to the next chapter, "Joomla Fields Explained", to learn how to make your articles far more interesting.

# CHAPTER 7.

## JOOMLA FIELDS EXPLAINED

---

This chapter explains how you can add interesting and useful data to your Joomla articles.

Joomla provides fields which you can use to show dates, numbers, images, URLs and much more.

After reading this chapter, you'll be able to do the following:

- Understand the different types of Joomla fields.
- Display the fields on your Joomla articles.

### INTRODUCING FIELDS

Often you write content that is very straightforward. Simple content doesn't need more than a title, plus some main text. That describes the articles we've been writing so far.

However, some content is more detailed.

For example, imagine you want to list businesses on your Joomla site. Each business requires a title and text, plus also a phone number, logo, address, and website link.

Or imagine that you want to display your company's products. Each product needs a price, photos, weight, and SKU number.

Fields enable you to create rich and detailed content in Joomla. Let's see how fields work. We're going to use the same CASh workflow that we've recommended throughout the book.

### Step #1. Categorize

With Fields, the organization we use is called Field Groups, rather than Categories.

- Go to "Content", then "Field Groups".
- Click "New".
- Title: **Attraction Details**
- Description: **These fields show information about Joomlaville attractions.**
- Click "Save & Close".

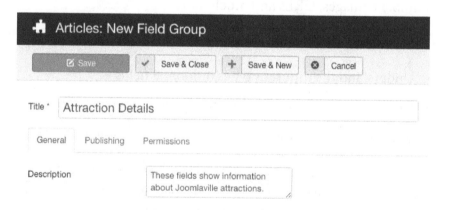

### Step #2. Add

Now let's create fields for the attractions. The first field will be a date field, showing when the attraction first opened.

- Go to "Content", "Fields", and click "New".
- Title: **Date Opened**
- Field: **Calendar**

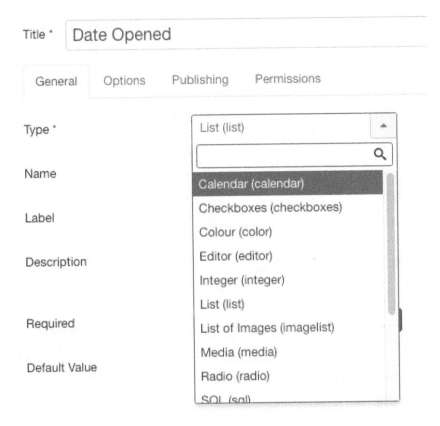

- Description: **This is when this attraction was first open to the public**.
- Required: **Yes**.

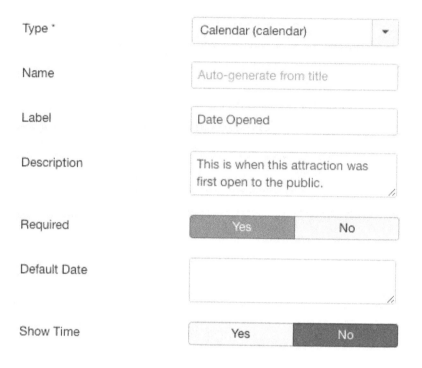

We also need to categorize this field correctly. On the right-hand side, choose these options:

- Field Group: **Attraction Details**
- Category: **Attractions**

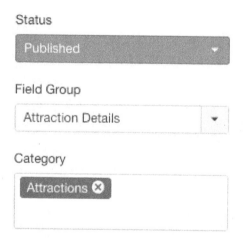

- Click "Save & Close" to complete the field.

The next field will be a list of amenities available for visitors to the attraction.

- Go to "Content", "Fields", and click "New".
- Title: **Amenities**
- Field: **List**

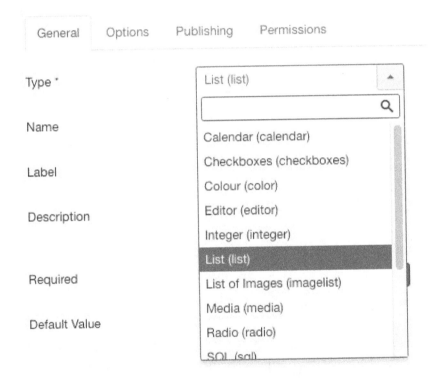

- Description: **These are the resources available to visitors**.
- Required: **Yes**
- Multiple: **Yes**

At the bottom of the screen, you'll see a "List Values" area:

List Values

- Click the green + icon and enter "Restaurant" into the Text field. This is what visitors will see.

- Also, fill in the "Value" field. This is the name Joomla will use to store the data so it doesn't have to be user-friendly.

List Values

| Text | Value | |
|------|-------|---|
| Restaurant | restaurant | |

- Repeat this process for "Gift Shop", "Picnic Areas", and "Restrooms".

List Values

| Text | Value | |
|------|-------|---|
| Restaurant | restaurant | |
| Gift Shop | gift shop | |
| Picnic Areas | picnic areas | |
| Restrooms | restrooms | |

- Field Group: **Attraction Details**
- Category: **Attractions**
- Click "Save & Close".

You've successfully added two fields. Let's see how we use them to show information to our website's visitors.

### Step #3. Show

In this step, we'll enter data for one of our attractions:

- Go to "Content", then "Articles".
- Open the "Museum" article.
- Click the "Attraction Details" tab:

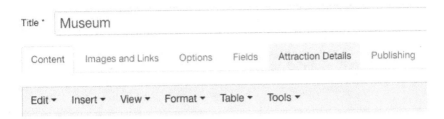

You should now see both of your fields as in the image below. If you don't see both fields, retrace your steps and make sure you have chosen the correct Field Group and Category for both fields.

- Click "Date Opened" and choose a date:

Date Opened *

Amenities *

- Click "Amenities" and choose several of the options:

Amenities *

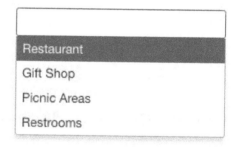

- When you're finished, your fields will look like this:

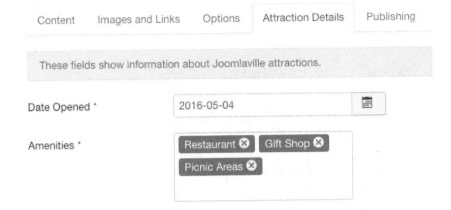

- Save this article and visit the front of your site. Click the "Attractions" tab and visit the Museum article. You'll see the fields on display:

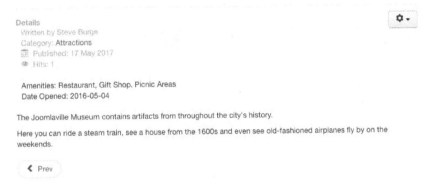

## MORE FIELD EXAMPLES

Now that we've seen one example of fields, let's see some more advanced examples. The first example will be a logo for our attractions.

- Go to "Content", "Fields", and click "New".
- Title: **Attraction Logo**
- Type: **Media**

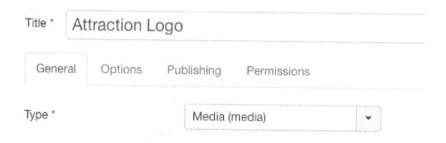

- Description: **This field contains the logo for this particular attraction.**
- Required: **Yes**
- Directory: **attractions**

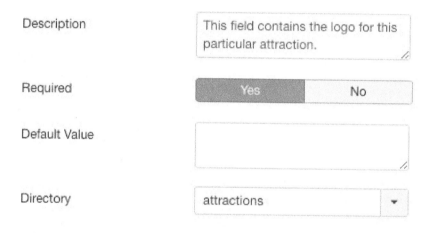

- Field Group: **Attraction Details**
- Category: **Attractions**
- Click "Save & Close".

Let's try that again, but this time we'll show a series of photos from the attraction:

- Title: **Attraction Photos**
- Type: **List of images**

- Description: **This field contains several photos for the attraction.**
- Required: **Yes**
- Directory: **attractions**
- Multiple: **Yes**
- Field Group: **Attraction Details**
- Category: **Attractions**
- Click "Save & Close".

Let's add the photos. You can download sample photos from https://ostraining.com/books/j3e/chapter7/.

- Go to "Content", "Articles", and open "Zoo".
- Add details for the Date Opened and Amenities fields.
- Click "Select" next to the Attraction Logo field.
- In the pop-up, click "Choose Files" and upload all the sample images you downloaded:

- After uploading, you'll see all four images have been added to the attractions folder:

Change Image

Folder

/attractions    ▾    Up

lemur.jpg    parrot.jpg    zebra.jpg    zoo.jpg

- Select the Zoo image and click "Insert".

Insert

zoo.jpg

- Next, you can add the three animal images to the "Attraction Photos" field. However, you may need to click "Save" for your new images to show. Here is how your screen will look after choosing the three images:

| Date Opened * | 2017-05-01 |
| Amenities * | Gift Shop ⊗  Picnic Areas ⊗ |
| Attraction Logo * | 👁  images/attractic  Select  ✖ |
| Attraction Photos * | lemur.jpg ⊗  parrot.jpg ⊗  zebra.jpg ⊗ |

Save the Zoo article, and visit the front of your site. Your Zoo article will look like the screenshot below:

## Zoo

Details
Written by Steve Burge
Category: Attractions
Published: 17 May 2017
Hits: 3

Date Opened: 2017-05-01
Amenities: Gift Shop, Picnic Areas

Attraction Logo:

Attraction Photos:

Great! Your fields are working. You've seen how many of Joomla's fields work. If you want a detailed explanation for all 15 fields, visit https://joomlashack.com/blog/tutorials/fields-joomla/.

However, it is time to do some cleaning up. The article display does not look as good as it should. The fields are not perfectly aligned, and there's too much clutter on the page.

## CLEANING UP OUR DISPLAY

First, let's make our fields look better. We don't need "Attraction Logo" or "Attraction Photos" to display on the page.

- Go to "Content", "Fields" and edit the "Attraction Logo" field.
- Click the "Options" tab.
- Set "Show Label" to "Hide".
- Set "Automatic Display" to "Before Title".

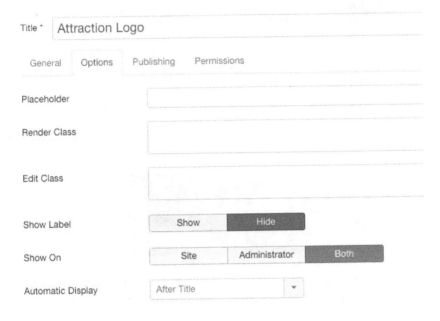

- Save this field and open the "Attraction Photos" field.
- Click "Options" again.
- Set "Show Label" to "Hide".
- Set "Automatic Display" to "After Display".

If you save this field and visit the front of your site, you'll see that your Zoo article looks considerably cleaner:

## Zoo

Details
Written by Steve Burge
Category: Attractions
Published: 17 May 2017
Hits: 5

Date Opened: 2017-05-01
Amenities: Gift Shop, Picnic Areas

Joomlaville Zoo is a wonderful place for families to visit.

There is an aviary for birds and a farm for animals like cows, pigs and geese.

The zoo also has exotic animals such as lions, tigers, giraffe and buffalo.

Overall, it's a great experience for young children.

❮ Prev                                                          Next ❯

However, there is more data that we can remove. For example, the Published date and the number of hits are not really important.

There are three levels we can target for turning off these features:

- The whole site
- The Attractions category
- The Zoo article

In this example, we're going to turn off these features for the whole site. In the next chapter, we'll look at how to make these choices for categories and articles.

- If you are anywhere under the "Content" menu, click the "Options" button in the top-right:

This page has a large number of configuration options for your content. On the first tab called "Articles", you'll see the options we need. Make these changes:

- Show Category: **Hide**
- Show Author: **Hide**
- Show Publish Date: **Hide**
- Show Navigation: **Hide**

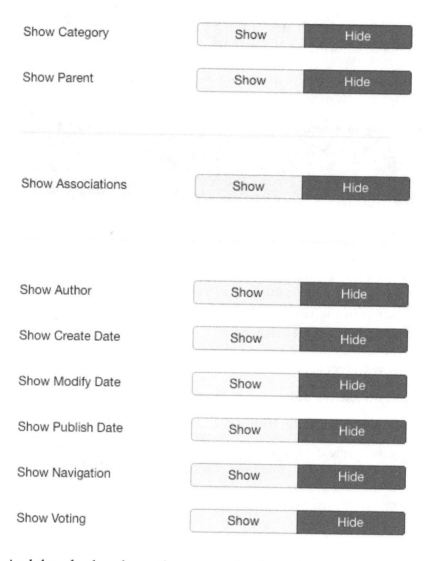

And then further down the page, make these changes too:

- Show Icons: **Hide**
- Show Print: **Hide**
- Show Email: **Hide**
- Show Hits: **Hide**

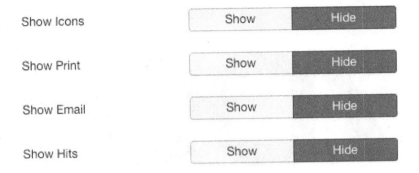

- Click "Save" and visit your Zoo article on the front of the site. The content should now be clean and stylish:

## Zoo

Date Opened: 2017-05-01
Amenities: Gift Shop, Picnic Areas

Joomlaville Zoo is a wonderful place for families to visit.

There is an aviary for birds and a farm for animals like cows, pigs and geese.

The zoo also has exotic animals such as lions, tigers, giraffe and buffalo.

Overall, it's a great experience for young children.

## WHAT'S NEXT?

We've added great articles to our site, but there's a problem. As we add more and more articles, it becomes harder to find them all.

We need some better navigation so that people can easily find all of our wonderful articles.

In Joomla, navigation is created with menus. So that's what we're going to do next. In the next chapter, we'll get a better understanding of menus and menu links so we can create really good navigation on our site.

Turn to the next chapter, "Joomla Menus Explained", to learn more about menus.

# CHAPTER 8.

## JOOMLA MENUS EXPLAINED

---

Joomla has menus for two really good reasons.

First, menu links allow visitors to find pages on your site. Without menus, all your visitors would be stuck on the home page. That means we must have menu links to all our important pages.

Second, in Joomla, menu links have substantial control over how your page is laid out and displayed.

In this chapter, you'll see that menu links follow the same CASh workflow that we've used throughout this book.

After reading this chapter, you'll be able to do the following:

- Understand how Joomla menus work
- Categorize your menu links
- Add your menu links
- Show your menus
- Understand more advanced menu layout options

## CATEGORIZING YOUR MENU LINKS

We've already created links to many of our articles in the Main

Menu, but there are more menus on our site. Let's see one of those menus in action.

- Use the Login Form module on the front of your site to log in:

- The Login Form module will change to showing your name and a "Log out" button. You'll also see a new "User Menu" module:

**User Menu**

Your Profile
Submit an Article
Site Administrator
Template Settings
Site Settings

**Login Form**

Hi Steve Burge,

Log out

These five links are helpful for your site's users.

- For example, click on "Your Profile", and you can update your account details:

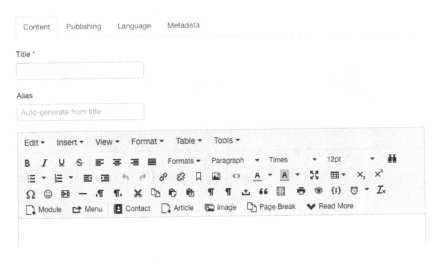

## Edit Your Profile

| | |
|---|---|
| Name * | Steve Burge |
| Username (optional) | steve |
| Password (optional) | |
| Confirm Password (optional) | |
| Email Address * | steve@ostraining.com |
| Confirm Email Address * | steve@ostraining.com |

- Click on "Submit an Article", and you have the ability to write articles from here. This feature makes it easy for users to write content without needing to log in to the administrator area.

We organized our articles using categories. We organize our menu links using menus.

- Go to the administrator area of your site and hover over "Menus". You'll see both "Main Menu" and "User Menu".

Let's see how to use the CASh workflow for menus. We're going to create a menu for our Information links. These are some of the most important articles about Joomlaville, so we want them available on every page.

### Step #1. Categorize

First, we'll create the menu to hold our Information links:

- Go to "Menus", "Manage", and then "Add New Menu":

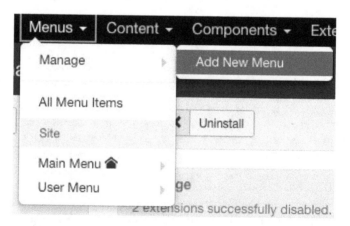

- Title: **Information Menu**

- Menu Type: **information**
- Description: **This menu has links to Information articles**
- Click "Save & Close".

## Step #2. Add

Now let's create links to our Information articles.

- Go to "Menus", "Information Menu", then "Add New Menu Item".

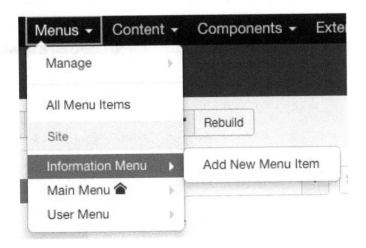

- Menu Title: **History**

- Menu Item Type: **Single Article**. You'll find this by clicking "Select" and then the Articles slider:

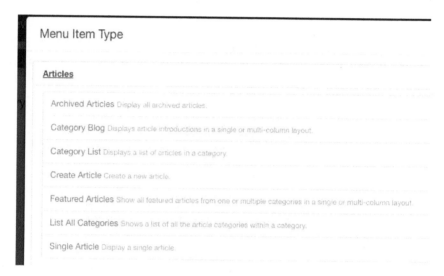

- Click "Select" next to "Select Article":

- Click "History". If it helps, you can use the search box in the pop-up window:

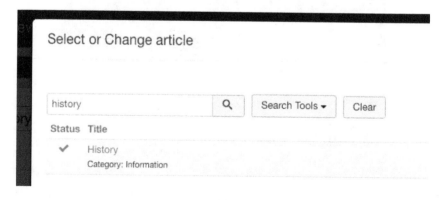

- Click "Save & Close".
- If you don't immediately see your new History link, use the dropdown filters to choose "Information Menu":

Let's repeat this process for our other two information articles:

- Go to "Menus", "Information Menu", then "Add New Menu Item".
- Menu Title: **Location**
- Menu Item Type: **Single Article**
- Select Article: **Location**
- Click "Save & Close".
- Repeat the process for the Climate article. When you're done, your list of menu links will look like this:

## Step #3. Show

At the moment, no-one can see our menu links, so let's make them visible. With menus, the "Show" part of the workflow is handled by modules.

- Go to "Menus", then "Manage".
- Click "Add a module for this menu".

You'll see a pop-up window.

- Title: **Joomlaville Information**
- Position: **Right**
- Click "Save & Close" in the bottom-right corner.

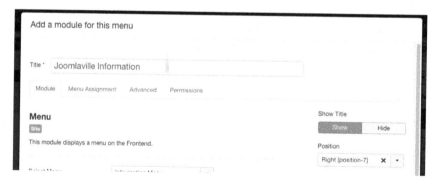

Visit the front of your site, and the new menu will appear on the right sidebar:

## DROPDOWN MENUS

Creating a new menu isn't the only way to organize your menu links. You can also add more links using dropdown links. These organize menu links and also help you to save space. Let's see how dropdown menus work, using the example of our Attraction links.

- Go to "Menus", "Main Menu", and then "Add New Menu Item".

- Menu Title: **Train Station**

- Menu Item Type: **Single Article**

- Select Article: **Train Station**

So far, we haven't done anything new. The trick when creating dropdown menus is to use the "Parent Item" option.

- In the "Parent Item" dropdown, choose "Transport":

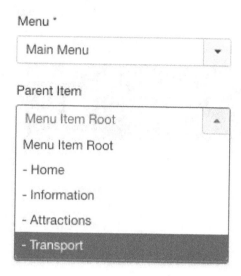

Menu *

Main Menu

Parent Item

Menu Item Root

Menu Item Root

- Home

- Information

- Attractions

- Transport

- Click "Save & Close" and visit the front of your site.
- Hover over the "Transport" link, and you'll see a "Train Station" dropdown.

# Joomlaville

Home    Information    Attractions    **Transport**

Train Station

Let's repeat that process for our other transport articles:

- Go to "Menus", "Main Menu", and then "Add New Menu Item".
- Menu Title: **Bus Station**
- Menu Item Type: **Single Article**

- Select Article: **Bus Station**

- Parent Item: **Transport**

- Click "Save & Close".

- Repeat for the Airport article.

When you're finished with these two new links, your menu will look this:

It's worth noting a couple of things about dropdown menus:

- Not all site designs (called "templates") support dropdown menus. We'll talk about this more in the chapter called "Joomla Templates Explained".

- It is possible to create more levels of dropdown menus, although this can get confusing. For example, if you edit your Airport article and choose "Bus Station" as the parent item, this is what you'll see:

# Joomlaville

Home   Information   Attractions   **Transport**

Train Station

Bus Station               Airport

## LAYOUT CHANGES

Until now, our category pages have all shared a standard layout.
There's one main article on the top row, and then two columns
underneath. This layout is controlled by the menu link.

### History

Joomlaville is a city with a rich history.

It started as a market town in the 17th century. The site was chosen because it was a major crossroads for people
traveling through the mountains.

As the city grew in the 19th and 20th centuries, more industries moved and people flocked to Joomlaville looking for
work. Many of our residents have now been here for several generations.

### Location

Joomlaville is in the southeast of our country, about a five
hour drive from the capital.

It is located near a large mountain range, so there is plenty
of opportunity for Joomlaville people to enjoy skiing,
kayaking and other outdoor activities.

Joomlaville is also about three hours from the beach, so
it's easy for residents to enjoy a sunny vacation.

### Climate

Joomlaville is a city located in a great climate at the
foothills of the mountains.

There is snow in the winter and plenty of sun during the
summer.

No matter time of year you visit, you'll find that Joomlaville
has enjoyable weather.

Let's see how to change this default layout.

- Go to "Menus", then "Main Menu".
- Click "Information".
- Click the "Blog Layout" tab. You'll see several options,
  including the ones in the image below:

Menu Title *  Information

Details    Category    **Blog Layout**    Options    Integration

If a field is left blank, global settings will be used.

# Leading Articles          Use Global (1)

# Intro Articles            Use Global (4)

# Columns                   Use Global (2)

# Links                     Use Global (4)

Notice the "Use Global" text? That means that these settings rely on the site-wide Options screen that we saw in "Joomla Fields Explained". We can override these settings on individual menu links.

If you're not sure what any of these options do, hover over the label and you'll see an explanation:

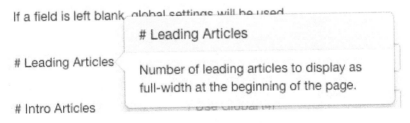

Let's turn the 1 row, 2 columns layout into a multiple row layout:

- # Leading Articles: **3**

Menu Title *   Information

Details      Category      **Blog Layout**      Options      Integration

If a field is left blank, global settings will be used.

\# Leading Articles                3

- Save the menu link and visit the front of your site. Click the "Information" link, and you'll see the layout has changed. There are now three articles full-width at the beginning of the page:

## History

Joomlaville is a city with a rich history.

It started as a market town in the 17th century. The site was chosen because it was a major crossroads for people traveling through the mountains.

As the city grew in the 19th and 20th centuries, more industries moved and people flocked to Joomlaville looking for work. Many of our residents have now been here for several generations.

## Location

Joomlaville is in the southeast of our country, about a five hour drive from the capital.

It is located near a large mountain range, so there is plenty of opportunity for Joomlaville people to enjoy skiing, kayaking and other outdoor activities.

Joomlaville is also about three hours from the beach, so it's easy for residents to enjoy a sunny vacation.

## Climate

Joomlaville is a city located in a great climate at the foothills of the mountains.

There is snow in the winter and plenty of sun during the summer.

No matter time of year you visit, you'll find that Joomlaville has enjoyable weather.

This was a relatively small change, but it is possible to make larger layout changes. In this example, we'll replace the blog layout with a table layout:

- Go to "Menus", then "Main Menu".
- Click "Attractions".

- Click "Select" next to "Menu Item Type".

- Choose "Category List":

You will have to select the Attractions category again after making this change:

- Choose a Category: **Attractions**

- Save the menu link and visit the front of your site. Click the "Attractions" link, and you'll see the layout has changed to a table format.

If you want to change the appearance of this table, you can edit the Attractions link again. The "List Layouts" tab will allow you to enable and disable features:

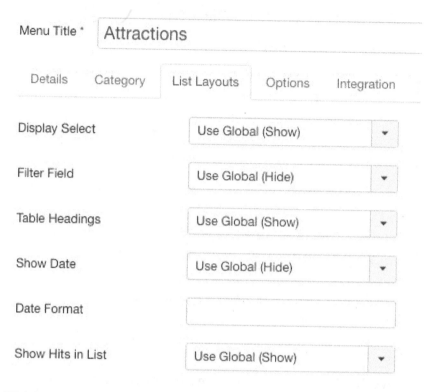

## PRACTICING THE CASH WORKFLOW

Over the course of the last few chapters, we've been explaining the CASh workflow.

Now that you understand more about menus, you're ready for a complete practice of the CASh workflow.

We're going to move through the CASh workflow, from start to finish. Here's the plan:

- Categorize: Categories
- Add: Articles
- Show: Menu links

We're going to use the example of parks in Joomlaville.

## Step #1. Categorize

First, let's create the category for our Parks:

- Go to Content, then Category Manager, and click New.
- Title: Parks
- Click "Save & Close". You should now have six categories, as shown in the figure below:

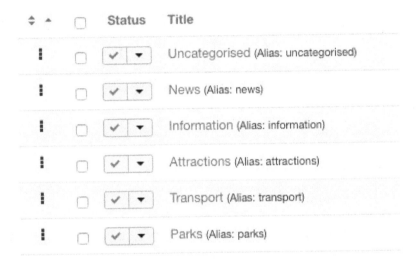

| | | Status | Title |
|---|---|---|---|
| ⋮ | ☐ | ✔ ▼ | Uncategorised (Alias: uncategorised) |
| ⋮ | ☐ | ✔ ▼ | News (Alias: news) |
| ⋮ | ☐ | ✔ ▼ | Information (Alias: information) |
| ⋮ | ☐ | ✔ ▼ | Attractions (Alias: attractions) |
| ⋮ | ☐ | ✔ ▼ | Transport (Alias: transport) |
| ⋮ | ☐ | ✔ ▼ | Parks (Alias: parks) |

We're also going to upload images for our Parks articles, so let's create the folder for them:

- Go to "Content", and then "Media".
- Click "Create New Folder" and create a folder called **Parks**.

## Step #2. Categorize

Second, let's write our Parks articles. All of the text and images are available at https://ostraining.com/books/j3e/chapter8/.

- Go to "Content", "Articles", and "Add New Article" to start the process.

- When you've added all three articles, use the Select Category filter to check that your Parks articles are correct. Your screen should look like the one below.

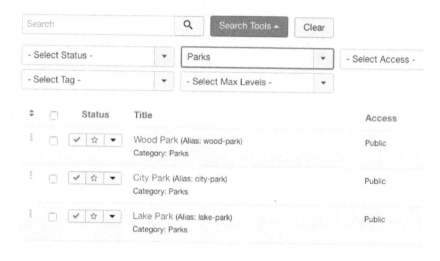

## Step #3. Show

Now let's go and make a menu for our news:

- Go to "Menus, "Main Menu", and click "Add New Menu Item".
- Title: **Parks**
- Menu Item Type: **Category List**
- Choose a Category: **Parks**
- Click "Save & Close" and visit the front of your site. Click the Parks menu link, and you should see the layout shown in the screen below.

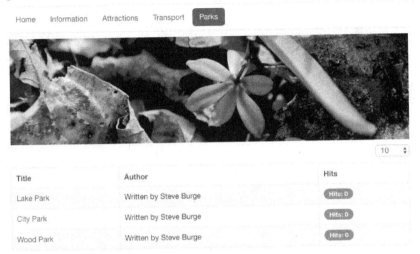

# Joomlaville

Home   Information   Attractions   Transport   Parks

| Title | Author | Hits |
|-------|--------|------|
| Lake Park | Written by Steve Burge | Hits: 0 |
| City Park | Written by Steve Burge | Hits: 0 |
| Wood Park | Written by Steve Burge | Hits: 0 |

Congratulations! You've just used the entire CASh workflow.

We absolutely recommend that you use the CASh workflow to set up your content. Nearly every time that we find someone who is confused about Joomla, it is because they didn't follow CASh:

- **Categorize**: If you don't use categories, you'll soon find that your articles are unorganized and difficult to manage.
- **Add**: If you don't add articles, you'll have an empty site.
- **Show**: If you don't have any menu links, people won't be able to see your content.

As you can see, if you skip any of these three steps, you'll be headed for trouble.

The same thing is true if you try these steps in a different order. For example, many people want to create menu links first. Often this is because they've used software like Dreamweaver before, and with Dreamweaver you do create the navigation first.

I'm not going to argue about whether Joomla is better than other software you've used before, but it's important to remember that Joomla is probably different and it requires a different approach.

The approach we recommend for Joomla is the CASh workflow.

WHAT'S NEXT?

Now that we've covered Content, we're going to turn our attention to Extensions, which are the extra features we can add on to our site.

Each time you were creating menu links in this chapter, you saw a screen like the one below. You undoubtedly noticed that you could link to many more things beyond just articles. In fact, you can link to Contacts, News Feeds, Search, Users, and much more.

## Menu Item Type

Articles

Configuration Manager

Contacts

News Feeds

Search

Smart Search

System Links

Tags

Users

Wrapper

In the next chapter, we show you what all those extra features are and how they can enhance your Joomla site. These extra features are a type of extension called Components. Turn the page and let's see how Components work.

# CHAPTER 9.

## JOOMLA COMPONENTS EXPLAINED

---

If you want to add an exciting extra feature to your site, there's a good chance it's a component. Do you want to show an advertising banner? That's a component. Want a contact form? That's a component too. How about an events calendar or a discussion forum? Both are components.

Joomla arrives with eleven default components such as advertising banners and contact forms. In this chapter, we show you how they work.

In a future chapter, "Adding Joomla Extensions Explained", we show you how to find and add extra components such as events calendars and discussion forums.

In this chapter, we'll go over the eleven default Joomla components:

1. **Banners:** Shows advertising banners.
2. **Contacts:** Creates contact forms.
3. **Joomla Update:** This allows you to update your site.
4. **Messaging:** Sends private messages to other site administrators.
5. **Multi-lingual Associations**: This feature helps if you're building a multi-lingual site.
6. **News Feeds:** Shows news from other websites.

7. **Post-installation Messages**: Shows information about what's included in new Joomla versions.
8. **Redirect:** Tracks when people try to visit pages that don't exist on your site and allows you to redirect them to the correct pages.
9. **Search:** Allows people to search your site.
10. **Smart Search:** Allows people to search your site in more advanced ways.
11. **Tags:** Allows you to organize your content in a more flexible way than categories.

BANNERS COMPONENT

The Banners component has two main tasks:

- It shows advertising banners.
- It collects all the data about those banners, such as the number of times each one has been shown and the number of times each one has been clicked on.

Banners uses the CASh workflow of Categorize, Add, Show. Let's use that workflow to add an advertising banner on our site.

Let's walk you through the process of setting up an advertising banner. Here's how we do it.

**Step #1. Categorize**

Just as with our articles, our banners are organized into categories. So we need to create a category for them:

- Go to "Components", then "Banners", and then "Categories":

The Banners categories will each be used for different areas of the site, so naming them according to their position (Leaderboard, Left Column, Right Column) is a good idea.

- Click "New".

- Let's create a banner for the right-hand side of our site, so enter **Right Column** into the Title field, as in the image below.

- Click "Save & Close" when you're finished.

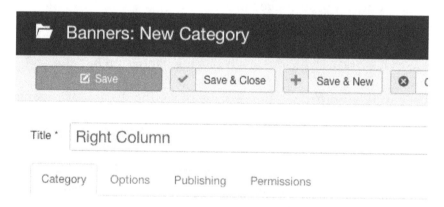

With the Banners, there's also a second method of organization called "Clients". This allows you to organize banners by advertising client. Why is this useful? You might want to sell banner space to several different clients and have an easy way to track all their banners. If you want to do this, the process of setting up a client is exactly the same as for a category.

## Step #2. Add

Now let's create the banner that visitors will see:

- Go to "Components, then "Banners".
- Click "New", and you see the banner setup page.
- Name: Give the banner a descriptive title. In this case, enter **Right Column Joomla.org Banner**.
- Image: Click "Select", and you see a pop-up. This takes you to the banners folder in Media Manager. You can upload a new advertising banner here or even browse to other folders. In this case, click on the image called "white.png", and then click "Insert".
- Click URL: This is the Web address to send people to when they click the banner. Let's put **http://www.joomla.org** in here.
- Category: Choose the **Right Column** category you created earlier.

## Step #3. Show

Now we just need to tell Joomla where to show the banner:

- Go to "Extensions", then "Modules", and click New.
- You see a screen where you can decide which type of module to create. Click "Banners".

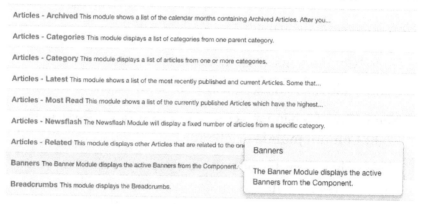

## Select a Module Type:

Articles - Archived This module shows a list of the calendar months containing Archived Articles. After you...

Articles - Categories This module displays a list of categories from one parent category.

Articles - Category This module displays a list of articles from one or more categories.

Articles - Latest This module shows a list of the most recently published and current Articles. Some that...

Articles - Most Read This module shows a list of the currently published Articles which have the highest...

Articles - Newsflash The Newsflash Module will display a fixed number of articles from a specific category.

Articles - Related This module displays other Articles that are related to the one

Banners The Banner Module displays the active Banners from the Component.

Breadcrumbs This module displays the Breadcrumbs.

> Banners
>
> The Banner Module displays the active Banners from the Component.

You see a screen like the one below. There are four key options to choose:

- Title: **Right Column Banner**
- Category: **Right Column**
- Show Title: **Hide**
- Position: **Right**

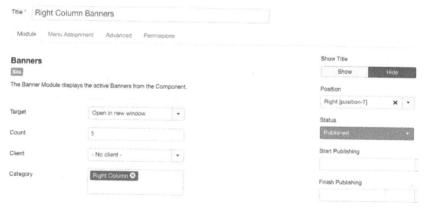

- Click "Save & Close" and visit your site. You can see the "SUPPORT Joomla" banner in the right column, as in the image below. Go ahead and click on the banner to test that it works. It should send you to http://joomla.org.

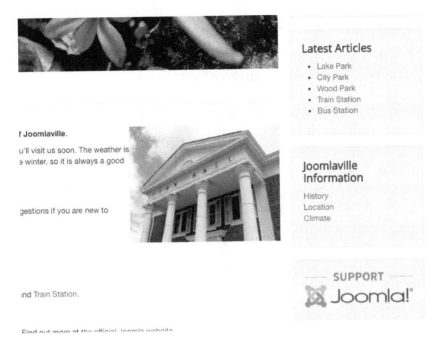

## Banner Data

Joomla can collect basic data about how often the banner is shown (Impressions) or how often it's clicked on (Clicks). Here's how you can start collecting that information:

- Go to "Components", then "Banners".

- You'll see that Joomla has started to track both the impressions and the click for this banner:

Please note that the data recorded for impressions and clicks is not accurate enough to replace any professional advertising systems. However, it does work well enough for the average user's needs.

## CONTACTS COMPONENT

The Contacts component has one main task: It allows visitors to contact you. You probably guessed that already!

Contacts allows you to easily set up forms. If you just want one contact form for the whole site, that's easily done. You can also set up a whole directory of contact forms for different people or different departments.

You can also create more advanced forms using the fields that we saw earlier in "Joomla Fields Explained".

The CASh workflow applies to contacts, just as much as for content, menus, and banners. We're going to Categorize, Add, and then Show. However, now that you understand the CASh workflow, we're going to show how to skip the first step.

### Step #1. Categorize

This time, we're going to combine Step 1 and Step 2. So we'll do the "Categorize" step in the instructions below.

### Step #2. Add

- Go to "Components", then "Contacts".
- Click "New".
- Name: **Joomlaville Mayor**
- Email: Enter your e-mail address into the Email field. This e-mail won't be made public, but whenever anyone uses the contact form, an e-mail gets sent to this address.
- Category: Type **Joomlaville Contacts** and then press "Enter" or "Return" on your keyboard. This is a faster way to complete Step #1.

Category *

- Uncategorised

Joomlaville Contacts                 🔍

Add new Category "Joomlaville
Contacts"

When all three fields are filled in, your screen should look like
the one below:

We're also going to make a small option change. This is a design
change because I personally think another layout is easier to read
than the default Contacts layout:

- Click the "Display" tab.

- Set the "Display Format" option to "Plain", as shown in the
  figure below:

## Step #3. Show

Now that you have your contact form ready, the final step is to make it publicly visible via a menu link. Because we already have a Contact Us menu link, we're going to edit that instead of adding a new link.

- Go to "Menus, "Main Menu", then "Add New Menu Item".
- Title: **Contact**
- Menu Item Type: **Single Contact**
- Select Contact: **Joomlaville Mayor**

Now visit the front of your site, and your contact form will look like the image below:

Joomlaville Mayor

Contact

Contact Form

If anyone uses this form, you will now get an email that looks like this:

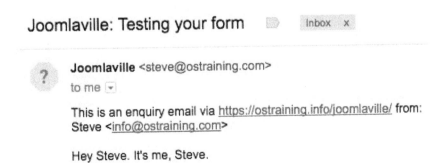

## Advanced Contact Options

There are some useful features you can use to improve your form. For example, you can add more data about your organization:

- Go to "Components", then "Contacts" and edit "Joomlaville Mayor".
- You will see a variety of contact fields, including Address, City or Suburb, State or Province, Telephone, and Website. The image below shows some sample data from OSTraining:

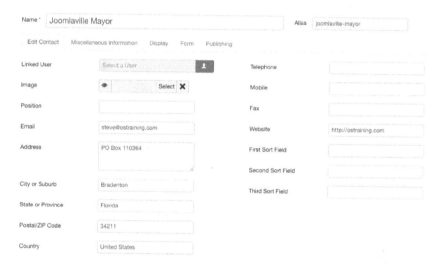

Here's how that data will appear on the front of the site:

# Joomlaville Mayor

## Contact

PO Box 110264
Bradenton
Florida
34211
United States
http://ostraining.com

## Contact Form

Send an Email

You can also create custom fields to improve this contact form. This process will be similar to the process we used in "Joomla Fields Explained", but there will be some small differences.

- Go to "Components" and "Contacts".
- Click "Field Groups" in the left-hand sidebar.
- This is the important new task: choose "Mail" from the dropdown menu. This means your fields will be attached to contact forms that users can rely on to send an email. If we choose "Contact" or "Category", our fields will only be available to site administrators.

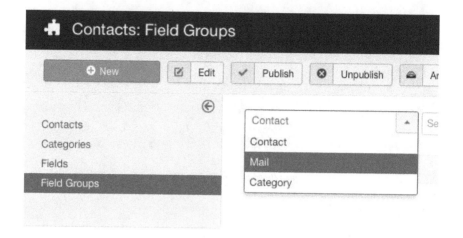

- Click "New".

- Title: **Extra Contact Details**

- Save the field group and make sure your next screen looks like this:

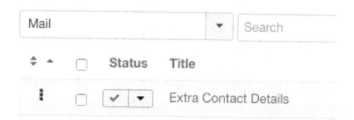

- Click "Fields" in the left-hand sidebar.

- Again, choose "Mail" in the dropdown menu:

- Click "New".
- Title: **What is Your Question About?**
- Type: **Checkboxes**

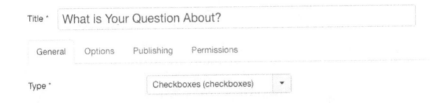

- Field Group: **Extra Contact Details**
- Checkbox Values: Enter topics that people might be contacting you about.

- Click the "Permissions" tab.

- Set "Edit Custom Field Value" to "Allowed". This will allow anyone to enter data into this field.

- Visit the front of your site, and your contact form will now have a custom field:

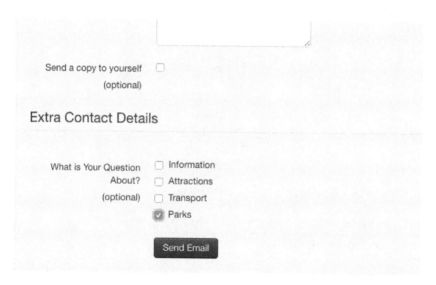

- Any fields you add using this method will get added to emails you receive:

## JOOMLA! UPDATE, MESSAGING, MULTI-LINGUAL ASSOCIATIONS AND POST-INSTALLATION MESSAGES

There are four components that we'll skip over in this chapter:

- Joomla! Update: We're going to come back and talk about this feature in the chapter called, "Joomla Site Management Explained".

- Messaging: This is one of the simplest components. It allows you to send private messages to other members of your site. However, it really does have very limited features and in many years of using Joomla, I've never seen it used on a real site.

- Multi-lingual Associations: This is very useful for multi-lingual sites, but that is not something we cover in this book. We hope to add a chapter on multi-lingual sites in a future update.

- Post-Installation Messages: This is another feature we'll talk about later in "Joomla Site Management Explained".

## NEWS FEEDS COMPONENT

The News Feeds component allows you to automatically show news from other websites.

News Feeds uses a technology called RSS or Real Simple Syndication to pull in the feeds from other sites.

Let's walk you through the process of setting up feeds on your site. We'll use our CASh workflow again.

### Step #1. Categorize

Just as with our articles, banners, and contacts, our news feeds are organized into categories:

- Go to "Components", "News feeds", and then "Categories".
- Click "New" and enter a general title for our category, such as **Joomla News**. Your screen looks like the one below:

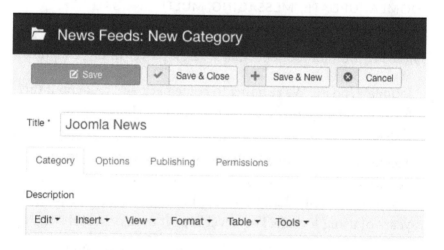

### Step #2. Add

Next, we need to find the feeds that we're going to import. The normal way to do this is to browse to the sites you're interested in and look for a little RSS icon. The common design for an RSS icon is a square image with a dot in the bottom-left corner and two waves coming out of it toward the top-right corner.

When looking for RSS feeds on other sites, you may need to hunt around a little as different sites put the feed in different places. Some put their RSS icon in the browser bar, some in the sidebar, and some in the site footer.

In this example, we're going to list the latest tutorials from Joomlashack.

- Go to "Components", "News Feeds", and then "Feeds".
- Click "New".
- Title: **Latest Joomlashack News**
- Link: **https://feeds.feedburner.com/jshack**
- Category: **Joomla News**

### Step #3. Show

All we need now is to make a menu link to our news feed:

- Go to "Menus", "Main Menu", then "Add New "Menu Item".
- Menu Title: **News**

- Menu Item Type: Click "Newsfeeds", then choose **Single News Feed**.

- Feed: Latest Joomlashack News

When you're finished, the front of your site will look like the image below:

## Latest Joomlashack News

The Joomlashack blog feed

1. How to Add Custom Fields to Joomla Contact Forms

With the arrival of custom fields in Joomla, it's now possible to create much more powerful contact forms.

I'll walk you through the basics of creating a Joomla contact form, and then you'll see how to add fields.

The examples in this tutorial are taken from the upcoming new version of "Joomla 3 Explained", the best-selling Joomla book.

2. What You Need to Know About Joomla 3.7.1

### REDIRECTS COMPONENT

The Redirects component records broken links that people try to visit on your site and allows you to safely redirect them to a working page.

Why would there be broken URLs on your site? There are two likely reasons:

- **Mistyped URL:** Someone may have mistyped the URL to one of your pages – it may even have been you. If this is the case, the location of the broken URL shows in the Referring Page column so you know where to go to fix the link.

- **Old URL:** If you moved your site to Joomla from another type of Web site, it's possible that your URLs have changed. People may still be trying to visit those old URLs.

The Redirects component is here to fix those links for you. It can automatically redirect broken URLs to a working URL of your choice.

Because the Redirects component isn't needed for every site, it isn't enabled by default. Here's how to enable Redirects:

- Go to "Extensions", then "Plugins".
- Type "Redirect" into the Search box, and you'll see the "System – Redirect" plugin:

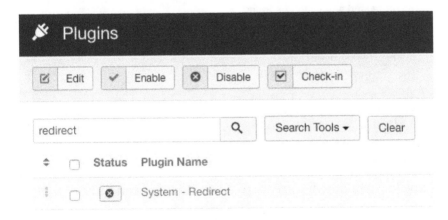

- Click the red X button. It will turn to a green check mark, and that will mean the plugin is enabled.

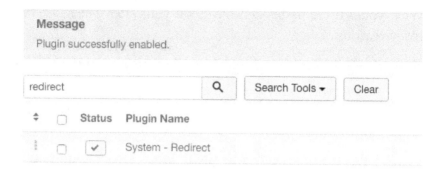

**Message**
Plugin successfully enabled.

| redirect | Q | Search Tools ▾ | Clear |
|---|---|---|---|

| ⬍ | ☐ | **Status** | **Plugin Name** |
|---|---|---|---|
| ⋮ | ☐ | ✔ | System - Redirect |

Now, let's generate some broken links so we can see how they are recorded by the Redirects component.

- Go to the front of your site.

- Try to access a broken URL. For example, click the "Contact" link. In the browser bar, delete the "act" from the end of the URL and try to access that URL. You know that you've found a broken link when you get a message saying "The requested page cannot be found", as in the image below:

Now let's see how Redirects recorded that broken link.

- Go to "Components", then "Redirects". You should see at least one recorded link, as in the image below:

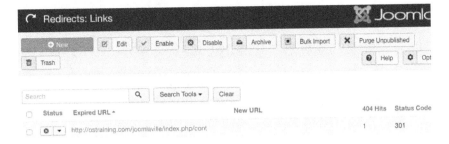

- Click on the broken URL.

- Destination URL: Enter the URL of the page you want people to be redirected to, as in the image below.

- Status: **Enabled**

Now you can test to see whether the redirect is working.

- Copy the Expired URL and paste it into the address bar of your browser. That broken URL should automatically redirect to the New URL. In this example, I could type in http://ostraining.com/joomlaville/index.php/cont and be automatically redirected to http://ostraining.com/ joomlaville/index.php/contact.

## THE SEARCH AND SMART SEARCH COMPONENTS

The Search component allows people to search for keywords on your site.

Of all the components introduced in this chapter, this is the one that is guaranteed to be used on almost every Joomla site.

Everything you need to use Search is already set up. There is a search form available on your site, as shown in the image below:

- Type "Joomlaville" into the search box and press Enter or Return on your keyboard. You see search results returned, as in the image below:

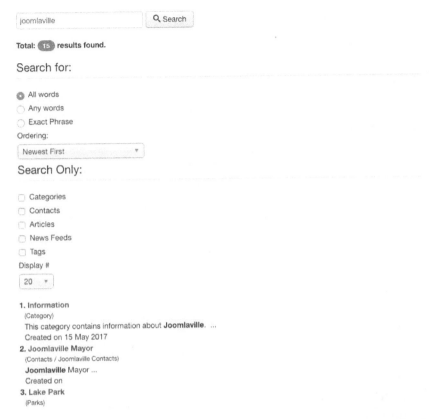

There aren't many settings you can configure for the Search component, but one is particularly useful. The "Gather Search Statistics" option allows you to track all the searches that people have made on your site. Those search results give you a good idea about what is popular or even what is hard to find on your site. Here's how to set it up:

- Go to "Components", then "Search".
- Click "Options" and set "Gather Search Statistics" to "Yes".

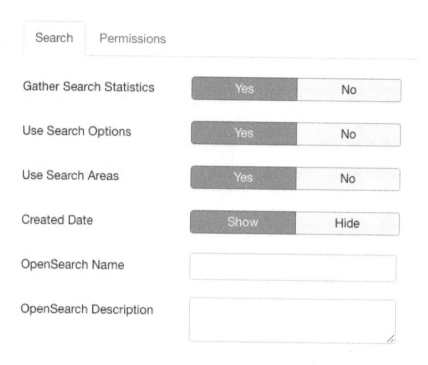

| | | |
|---|---|---|
| Search | Permissions | |
| Gather Search Statistics | Yes | No |
| Use Search Options | Yes | No |
| Use Search Areas | Yes | No |
| Created Date | Show | Hide |
| OpenSearch Name | | |
| OpenSearch Description | | |

Now whenever someone uses your site's search, it is recorded here inside the Search component, as in the image below. I've used the search box several times to show you how it works.

| Search Phrase | Hits ⌃ | Results |
|---|---|---|
| joomla | 1 | 18 |
| joomlaville | 2 | 15 |

The Smart Search component is a more sophisticated alternative to the Search component. It does allow you to search with more accuracy, but it has another useful feature if you're a Joomla beginner: it allows you to show your content in more advanced ways.

Here's how we set it up:

- Go to "Extensions", then "Plugins".
- Search for and enable the "Content – Smart Search" plugin.

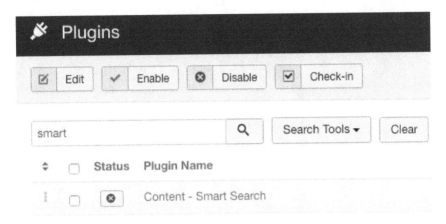

- Go to "Components", then "Smart Search".
- Click the "Index" button in the top-left corner, as shown in the image below.

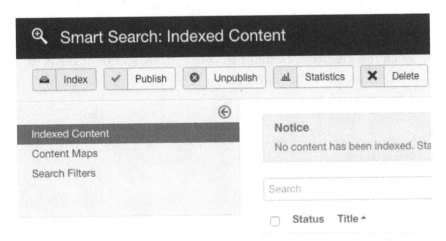

- You'll now see a pop-up box, and shortly afterwards you'll see a message saying "Indexing Complete".
- Close the window, and you'll see that Smart Search now has a list of all your content, as in the image below. In the future,

every time you add content, Smart Search will automatically add it to this index.

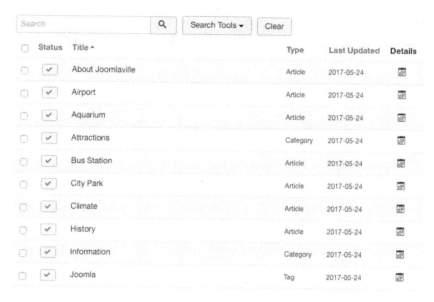

Now that Smart Search is ready, let's make it available to our site's users.

- Go to "Extensions", then "Modules".
- Click the green check mark next to Search, so that it turns to a red cross, as in the figure below. This will unpublish the default Search box.

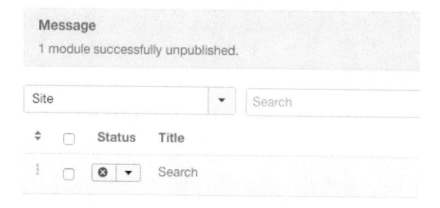

Now we're going to replace the Search box with a new Smart Search box:

- Click "New".
- Click "Smart Search".
- Title: **Smart Search**
- Search Field Label: **Hide**
- Show Title: **Hide**
- Position: **Search [position-0]**

- Visit the front of your site. You'll see what seems to be an unchanged search box. However, if you start typing, this new Smart Search feature will automatically recommend results, as in the image below.

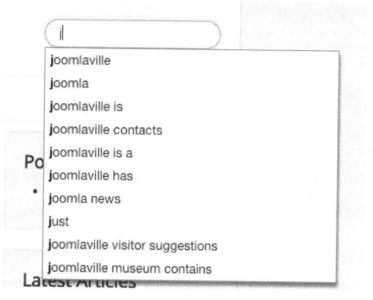

- Choose one of the search options. You'll find that the results are different than with the basic search. The Smart Search results are shown in the image below.

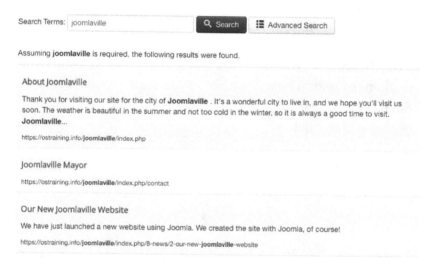

- Also, if you click on the "Advanced Search" button at the top of the search results, you'll see many more ways to find content. As shown in the image below, you'll see that you can search by Author, by Category, and by multiple other filters.

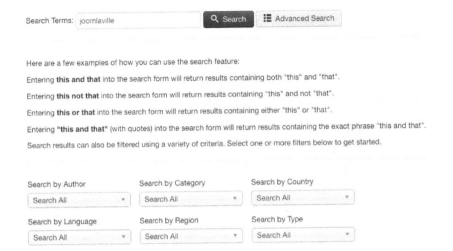

Here are a few examples of how you can use the search feature:

Entering **this and that** into the search form will return results containing both "this" and "that".

Entering **this not that** into the search form will return results containing "this" and not "that".

Entering **this or that** into the search form will return results containing either "this" or "that".

Entering **"this and that"** (with quotes) into the search form will return results containing the exact phrase "this and that".

Search results can also be filtered using a variety of criteria. Select one or more filters below to get started.

Smart Search looks wonderful, right? Why on earth would you not rush out and make it the default on your site?

There's only one real reason why you might avoid it: Smart Search doesn't support every extension. It does support all of the default extensions in this chapter, but in "Adding Joomla Extensions Explained" you will see how to add hundreds of new extensions. Smart Search doesn't support all of those extra extensions.

TAGS COMPONENT

The Tags component is a flexible and useful alternative to categories.

Throughout this book, we've used categories to organize our content. I still recommend that you continue to use categories, but there's no denying that Tags will allow you to do things that categories will not.

Let's go to the front of our site, and you'll see a "Popular Tags" module in the right-sidebar. If you click "Joomla" in the menu, you'll see all articles with that tag:

### Popular Tags

- Joomla

### Latest Articles

- Lake Park

At the moment, only one article has the Joomla tag: About Joomlaville. If you look closely at that article, you'll see the Joomla tag in the top-left corner:

### About Joomlaville

**Thank you for visiting our site for the city of Joomlaville.**

It's a *wonderful city* to live in, and we hope you'll visit us soon. The weather is beautiful in the summer and not too cold in the winter, so it is always a good time to visit.

### Joomlaville Visitor Suggestions

Joomlaville has lots to do. Here are some suggestions if you are new to Joomlaville.

You can visit:

- the Aquarium
- the Zoo
- the Museum

What if we wanted to create a list of places in Joomlaville that were suitable for young children?

Joomla only allows us to place articles in one category, so if we wanted to create a list of places that are suitable for kids, we couldn't use it for both Parks or Attractions. That is the problem that Tags can solve. It allows us to organize content in more sophisticated ways than categories. Do as follows:

- Go to "Content", then "Articles".
- Open the "Museum" article.

- In the Tags box, type in "Child Friendly" and press Return or Enter on your keyboard. You know that the Tag has been successfully created when it appears as it does in the screen below:

- Save the Zoo article, then add the Child Friendly tag to these articles: Lake Park and City Park. As you add the tags to those other articles, you'll notice that Joomla automatically completes the tag for you.

Now let's allow visitors to find our Child Friendly content:

- Go to "Menus", "Main Menu" and then "Add New Menu Item".
- Menu Title: **Child Friendly**
- Menu Item Type: choose "Tags", then **Tagged Items**
- Tag: **Child Friendly**
- Parent Item: **Attractions**
- Visit the front of your site and under Attractions, you'll find the Child Friendly page, which looks like the image below. On this page, you'll see that you've included content from two different categories.

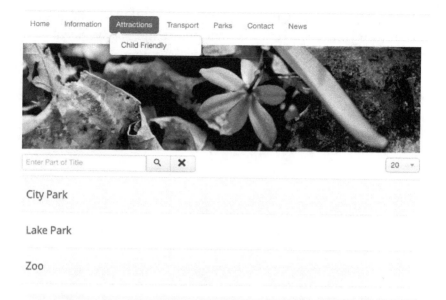

City Park

Lake Park

Zoo

So Tags are more flexible than categories because an article can have multiple tags, but only one category. Tags are also more flexible because they apply to articles, but also to Banners, Contacts, News Feeds, Users and more. With tags, you can organize almost anything on your site and place it on the same page.

As you've seen, you can create tags from inside your articles. The area inside Components, then Tags, is to provide one central place to control all of the tags on your site. Here you can edit, delete, rename and reorder all of your tags.

At the end of this chapter, your Joomlaville site will look similar to the image below. Don't worry if your site is not 100% identical to the image. The goal I have for you is to not perfectly re-create this site about Joomlaville. The goal is for you to understand the concepts and the processes that will help you to master Joomla. If you now feel comfortable creating banners, contact forms, search boxes, tags, and more, that's great: You're ready to move on to the next chapter.

## WHAT'S NEXT?

In this chapter, we introduced components, which add exciting extra features to your Joomla site.

Components are just one of several types of extensions that you can use to improve your Joomla site.

In "Joomla Modules Explained", you learn about another type of extension: modules. We've already talked about modules several times in this book.

Modules allow us to show small but important blocks of

information to our visitors. Turn the page and let's see how useful they can be.

# CHAPTER 10.

# JOOMLA MODULES EXPLAINED

---

Modules make life easier for our site's visitors. Modules are small blocks that allow visitors to quickly find information, links, or features. Because they're small, they're often found around the edges of your site's page.

In this chapter, you're going to create modules, and you'll also see three ways in which you can control modules. You'll learn how to:

- Change the position of modules
- Change the order that modules appear in
- Change menu links that modules appear on

## UNDERSTANDING MODULES

Modules normally go around the left, right, top, and bottom of your site. The default Joomla template has more than a dozen different places where you can place them. It is possible to get a visual guide to your template's module positions:

- Go to "Extensions", "Templates", and then "Templates".
- Click "Options" and set "Preview Module Positions" to "Enabled".
- Click "Save & Close".

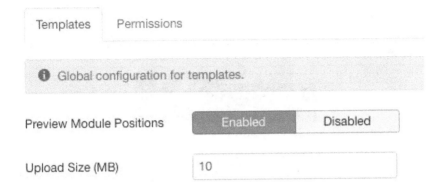

Templates      Permissions

ⓘ Global configuration for templates.

Preview Module Positions      | Enabled | Disabled |

Upload Size (MB)              | 10 |

- Scroll down and click the "Preview" link next to Protostar Details and Files, as shown in the image below. Protostar is the name of the template that we've been using so far in this book.

Protostar Details and Files          1.0        4/30/2012        Kyle Ledbetter
Preview                                                         admin@joomla.org

- You now see the template we've been looking at throughout the book, but you also now see the various module positions it contains, as shown in the image below:

# Joomlaville

Position: position-0 [ Style: none outline]

Home   position-1 [ Style: none outline]   Transport   Parks   Contact   News

Position: banner [ Style: xhtml outline]

Position: position-8 [ Style: xhtml outline]   Position: position-3 [ Style: xhtml outline]

Position: position-7 [ Style: well outline]
## Popular Tags
- Child Friendly
- Joomla

## About Joomlaville

Joomla

**Thank you for visiting our site for the city of Joomlaville.**

It's a *wonderful city* to live in, and we hope you'll visit us soon. The weather is beautiful in the summer and not too cold in the winter, so it is always a good time to visit.

### Joomlaville Visitor Suggestions

Joomlaville has lots to do. Here are some suggestions if you are new to Joomlaville.

You can visit:

- the Aquarium
- the Zoo
- the Museum

You can get here via the Airport, Bus Station and Train Station.

### Who Lives in Joomlaville?

Joomlaville is full of people who love Joomla! Find out more at the official Joomla website.

Position: position-2 [ Style: none outline]
You are here:  Home

Position: position-7 [ Style: well outline]
## Latest Articles
- Lake Park
- City Park
- Wood Park
- Train Station
- Bus Station

Position: position-7 [ Style: well outline]
## Joomlaville Information
History
Location
Climate

Position: position-7 [ Style: well outline]
SUPPORT
Joomla!

Position: position-7 [ Style: well outline]
## Login Form

Not every template is going to have the same layout. For example, let's look at Beez3, which is the other template provided by Joomla:

- Go back to the Templates screen.

- Click "Preview" next to Beez3 Details and Files.

| Image | Template ▲ | Version | Date | Author |
|---|---|---|---|---|
| | Beez3 Details and Files<br>Preview | 3.1.0 | 25 November 2009 | Angie Radtke<br>a.radtke@derauftritt.de<br>http://www.der-auftritt.de |

- The screen below shows module positions in the Beez3 template:

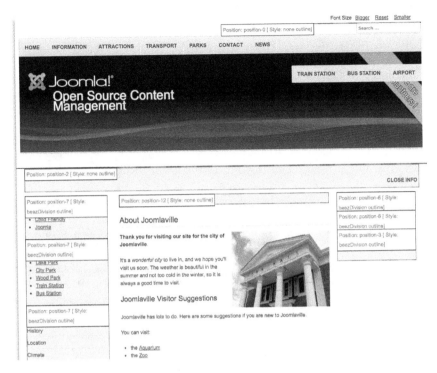

It is possible to get many more templates for Joomla. In most cases, the designer of a template will provide you with a map of the different module positions. For example, visit https://unlimited.joomlatemplate.joomlashack.com and you'll see a Joomla template called Unlimited.

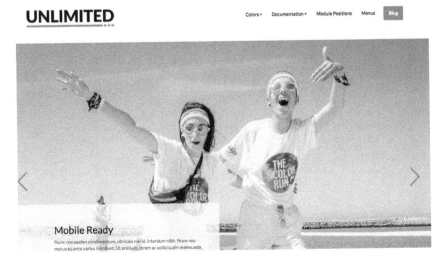

- Click the "Module Positions" link in the menu:

  Colors ▾     Documentation ▾     Module Positions     Menus     Blog

- You'll see a visual explanation of module positions with live examples:

- You'll see a large image that shows each module position:

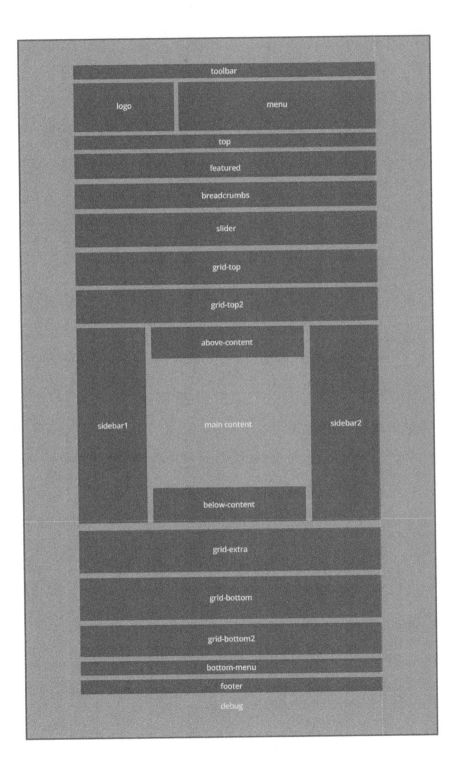

So, when you decide where to place modules on your site, it's important to understand what positions are available to you.

In the chapter "Joomla Templates Explained", we'll show you how to find new templates. Hopefully, whenever you find a template, there will be a grid showing all the module positions, like the images we've just seen. However, if there isn't, you can always go to the Template Manager and click on "Preview".

Now, let's put that new knowledge into action and place modules into those positions.

## CREATING NEW MODULES

In this book, we've often talked about Joomla's CASh workflow:

- Categorize
- Add
- Show

Modules are one way you can complete part 3 of the workflow: Show. For example, we could create a module that shows a list of popular articles on our site. This will be useful to visitors because they won't have to go searching around to find out what's interesting to people. Here's how that would fit into the CASh workflow:

- Categorize: Create categories for the articles.
- Add: Create articles.
- Show: Create the Popular Articles module.

Making this module is easy because in previous chapters we already completed Step 1 and Step 2 by creating the categories and articles. All that's left is to show.

Let's go and create that new module to show our visitors the most popular articles:

- Go to "Extensions", "Modules", and then click "New" in the top-left corner.
- Click "Articles – Most Read", as in the image below:

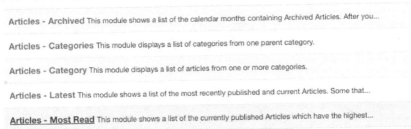

- Title: **Popular Articles**
- Position: **Right [position-7]**

- Click "Save & Close" and then visit your site. You see your new module on your front page, as in the image below:

Hopefully, you agree the process was straightforward. We can now leave this module alone because it will update automatically, based on the number of visitors to each article.

## CHANGING THE POSITION AND ORDER OF MODULES

As you can see, the right sidebar of our site is getting busy with six different modules. Let's clear that up and move some modules to other positions.

- Go to "Extensions", "Modules", and then click "Latest Articles".
- Change the Position dropdown to Left [position-9].

- Save the module and visit your site. The Latest Articles module has jumped to the left sidebar. Notice that the design of the module has changed: different module positions do have different designs for the modules inside them.

Now you know how to create Joomla modules and place them

in different positions on your site. However, what happens when you have multiple modules in one position? For example, you might decide that the Popular articles module should be on top of the right sidebar. Let's see how to do that:

- Go to "Extensions" and "Modules". You'll see a list of all your modules.

- In the "Select Position" dropdown, choose **position-7**. This will show only modules in the right sidebar.

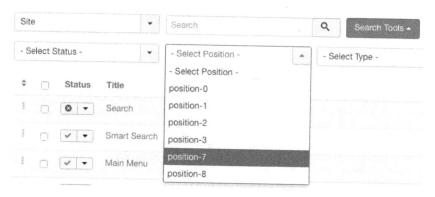

- Let's change this list of modules so that they are sorted in the order that they appear. Use the pulldown menu in the top-right corner to choose "Ordering ascending":

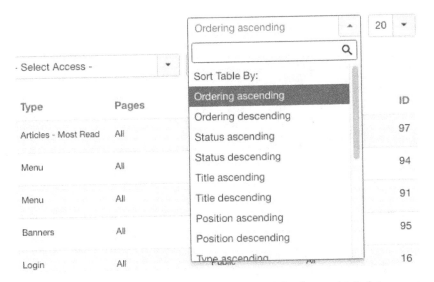

| Type | Pages | | ID |
|------|-------|---|-----|
| | Sort Table By: | | |
| Articles - Most Read | All | Ordering ascending | 97 |
| | | Ordering descending | |
| Menu | All | Status ascending | 94 |
| | | Status descending | |
| Menu | All | Title ascending | 91 |
| | | Title descending | |
| Banners | All | Position ascending | 95 |
| | | Position descending | |
| Login | All | Type ascending | 16 |

- To re-arrange the modules, select the black vertical dots. Holding those black vertical dots, you can drag-and-drop the module into a different position. The module will turn green while you are re-ordering it:

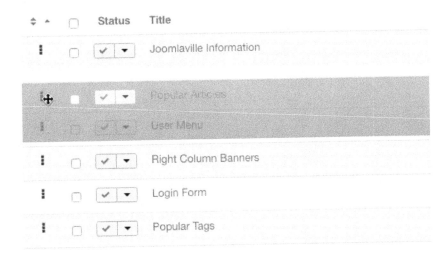

- See if you can re-order your modules so that the Popular Articles module is on top of the right sidebar:

## Popular Articles

- About Joomlaville
- Zoo
- Museum
- Lake Park
- Our New Joomlaville Website

## Joomlaville Information

History
Location
Climate

## CHANGING WHICH PAGES MODULES APPEAR ON

It is possible to have different modules appear when you click different menu links. Why would you want to do this? For example, if people visit your Attractions category, you can show them your latest attractions, and if people visit your Parks category, you can show them a module with a list of the Joomlaville parks. If every module appeared on all pages, things would quickly become messy!

Let's use the example of Parks. We will make a module that automatically updates with a list of all the parks in our city. Here's how we do it:

- Go to "Extensions", "Modules", and then click on "New".
- Choose "Articles Category" as the module type.
- Title: **Joomlaville Parks**

- Position: **Left [position-8]**
- Click the "Filtering Options" tab. Delete "All Categories" and choose "Parks" instead, as shown in the image below.

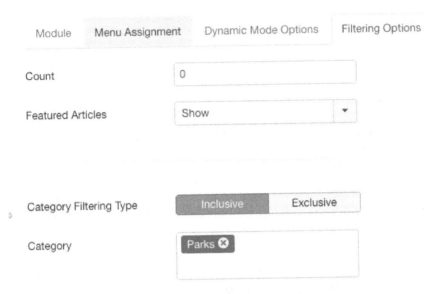

- Click on the "Menu Assignment" tab.
- Click the "Module Assignment" pulldown and choose "Only on the pages selected":

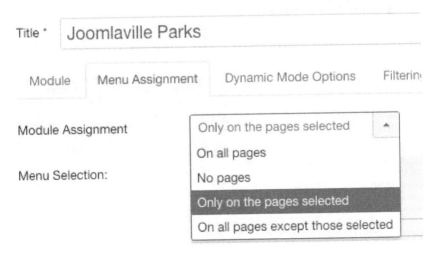

- We don't want this module to appear on most pages, so let's clear all of the check-boxes. Click the "None" button at the top of the menu link list, next to "Select":

Module Assignment     Only on the pages selected     ▼

Menu Selection:     Select: All, None | Expand: All, None

- Now check the box next to Parks:

☑ **Parks** (Alias: parks)

☐ **Contact** (Alias: contact)

☐ **News** (Alias: news)

- Click "Save & Close", then visit your site and click "Parks" in your Main Menu. Your new Joomlaville Parks module should appear on this page and no others.

Let's do that one more time to practice how it works.

Throughout this book we've been looking at the flower image on top of our content. Let's replace that image and make sure that it only appears on our homepage:

- Go to "Extensions", "Modules".
- Click "Clear" to remove any filters from earlier in the chapter.

- Click "Image Module" to open that module.
- Delete the existing green image and replace it with the homepage banner from https://ostraining.com/books/j3e/chapter9/.

- This is how your module will look after uploading that image:

**Custom**

`Site`

This module allows you to create your own Module using a WYSIWYG editor.

- Click the "Menu Assignment" tab and choose "Only on the pages selected".

- Click "None".

- Choose "Home".

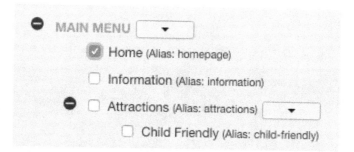

- Click Save & Close, then visit your site. Your new banner should only appear on the front page, as in the image below.

So, in this chapter you've learned how to control where modules appear, what order they are in, and what pages they appear on:

- **Position:** right, left etc.
- **Order:** first, second, third inside their module position.
- **Pages:** Which menu links you click to make them appear.

Wonderful! You have practiced, and you understand three ways that you can control modules on your Joomla site. In this chapter and in previous chapters, you've seen examples of some default Joomla modules, such as:

- Articles – Category
- Articles – Latest
- Articles – Most Read
- Banners
- Custom HTML
- Latest News
- Login
- Menu

- Tags – Popular
- Search
- Smart Search

By the end of this chapter, your site should look similar to the image below. Don't worry if your site doesn't look exactly like this one. So long as you understand the three ways to control a module on your site, you're ready to move on to the next chapter.

## WHAT'S NEXT?

You've now worked with two types of Joomla extensions. You

saw components that add large extra features, such as advertising banners and contact forms. You also saw modules that add small blocks of information around the outside of our site.

We're now going to look at plug-ins, which are the smallest extensions of all. They are Joomla's tiny helpers. Each one has a small task that it completes, such as allowing your visitors to vote on articles or including social bookmarking links in articles.

Turn the page and find out more about them.

# CHAPTER 11.

## JOOMLA PLUGINS EXPLAINED

---

Plugins are tiny but useful additions to your site. Each plugin does one simple thing. For example, one plugin allows your visitors to vote on articles you've written. Another plugin stops any e-mail address on the site from being collected by spammers.

After reading this chapter, you'll understand plugins, and be able to use them.

Plugins are the easiest thing we're going to do in this book! Why? Because at the beginner level you don't need to do much more than understanding them and using them. Most of them are so simple that they just need to be turned on or off, and they are ready.

- Go to "Extensions", then "Plugins", and you see a page like this one:

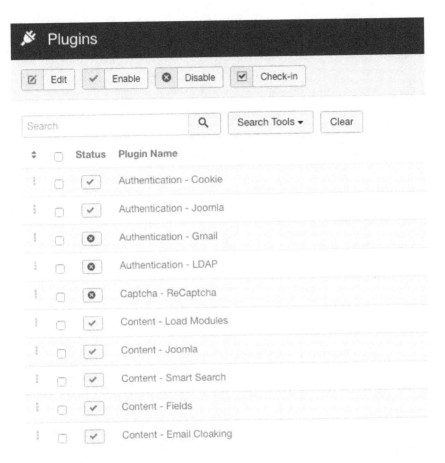

There are seventy-eight plugins here. Because plugins are so small and numerous, they even have their own categories. We introduce you to plugins by using some of these categories. By default, there are fourteen plugin categories, but we're going to focus only on the categories that you are most likely to use.

## AUTHENTICATION PLUGINS

Authentication is another word for "login." These plugins give you a variety of ways to log in to your Joomla site.

- Click on the "Select Type" pulldown menu, and choose "Authentication":

- When you've done that, you see four plugins:

The "Authentication – Joomla" plugin allows you to log in using your account on this Joomla site. For obvious reasons, please don't disable this particular plugin. You won't be able to log in again if you do.

There are two disabled plugins here: "GMail" and "LDAP". If you enable these plugins, here's what they'll do:

- **GMail:** If you enable this plugin, people will be able to log in to your Joomla site with their Google.com account details. There are some limitations to this, especially if you have extra security precautions on your Google account.

- **LDAP:** This plugin is much geekier. LDAP is a popular form of a user database often used on corporate networks. If you have a list of users in the LDAP format, you can enter the database details here, and Joomla allows those users to log in to your site, again on a temporary basis.

Extra authentication plugins are available that allow people to log in using their account on other popular platforms, such as

Twitter, Facebook, and OpenID. In the chapter called "Adding Joomla Extensions Explained," we show you how to add those to your site.

## CONTENT PLUGINS

Content plugins are those that directly affect your articles. These are probably the plugins that you will use most often.

Let's see the default content plugins. Click on the "Select Type" pulldown menu and choose "Content". You'll see nine plugins:

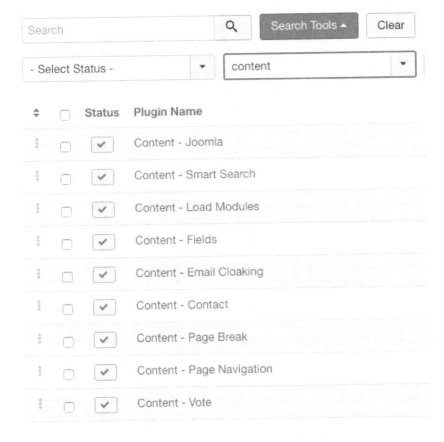

Let's take a look at what some of these content plugins do:

- **Joomla:** This plugin performs some maintenance tasks for your articles, such as emailing you if a new one is added.
- **Smart Search:** This helps the Smart Search component to create an index of your content.
- **Load Modules:** This plugin allows you to place modules inside your articles.

Wait? The Load Modules allows you to put modules inside of articles? Why would you want to do this? Because placing modules inside content can make them easier to find. Here's how we do it:

- Go to the Articles screen and open the "About Joomlaville" article.
- Enter a heading "**What Are People Looking for in Joomlaville?**". Use the Heading 3 format.
- Enter text, "These are some popular articles on our site:"

> You can get here via the Airport, Bus Station and Train Station.
>
> **Who Lives in Joomlaville?**
>
> Joomlaville is full of people who love Joomla! Find out more at the official Joomla website.
>
> **What Are People Looking for in Joomlaville?**
>
> These are some popular articles on our site:

- Place the cursor under your new text.
- Click the "Module" button in the toolbar:

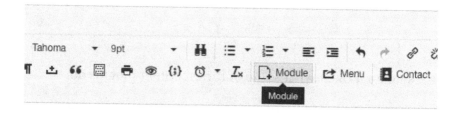

- In the pop-up window, click the "Popular Articles" button:

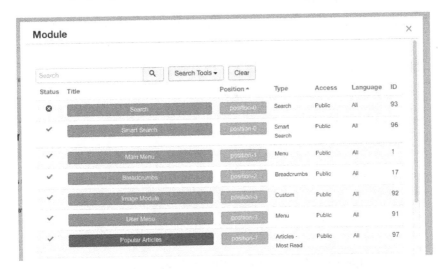

- Joomla will add syntax to your article that looks like this:

**Who Lives in Joomlaville?**

Joomlaville is full of people who love Joomla! Find out more at the official Joomla website.

**What Are People Looking for in Joomlaville?**

These are some popular articles on our site:

{loadmodule mod_articles_popular,Popular Articles}

- Save the article and go to the visitors' area of your site. Your homepage content should now include a working module:

## Who Lives in Joomlaville?

Joomlaville is full of people who love Joomla! Find out more at the official Joomla website.

## What Are People Looking for in Joomlaville?

These are some popular articles on our site:

## Popular Articles

- About Joomlaville
- Zoo
- Museum
- Lake Park
- Our New Joomlaville Website

What about some of the other content plugins?

- **Email Cloaking:** This plugin automatically hides e-mail addresses on your site from spammers. If you place your e-mail address in an article, it still looks like a normal e-mail address. In fact, it still acts like a normal e-mail address: If people click on it, their computer automatically creates an e-mail for them to send to you. The difference is, if this plugin is enabled, anyone trying to copy your e-mail gets a bunch of unreadable code.

- **Page Break:** The Page Break button allows you to split very long articles into multiple pages. If you use the Page Break inside an article, your content will have a small table of contents, as shown below:

# About Joomlaville

Joomla

Page 1 of 3
**Thank you
for visiting
our site for
the city of
Joomlaville**
.

It's a
*wonderful
city* to live
in, and we

About Joomlaville

Page 2

Page 3

All Pages

- **Page Navigation:** If you have many articles in one category, this plugin creates "Prev" and "Next" buttons so you can navigate between them. You can see an example in the image below:

## Bus Station

The Bus Station is a very good way to get to cities around Joomlaville.

The buses leave Joomlaville every hour on weekdays and every two hours on weekends.

**❮ Prev**     **Next ❯**

You are here: Home ▸ Transport ▸ Bus Station

- **Vote:** This plugin does exactly what its name suggests: It allows people to vote on your articles.

Here's how you can see the voting plugin in action:

- Go to "Content", "Articles" and open the "Wood Park" article.
- Click the "Options" tab and scroll down until you can set "Show Voting" to "Show".

- Repeat this for your other two Parks articles: Lake Park and City Park.
- Visit the front of your site, click "Parks" in the menu, and you'll now be able to vote on each park, as in the image below:

## Lake Park

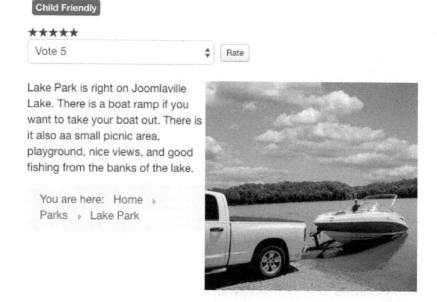

This is not very sophisticated voting. For example, it won't prevent determined people from voting multiple times. Nevertheless, it's a fun extra feature that you can turn on. Just don't forget to turn this off for certain articles using the Options area. For example, you don't want people voting on your staff member profiles!

## EDITORS AND EDITORS-XTD PLUGINS

Content plugins affect how your articles look in the visitors' area of your site.

**Editors** and **Editors-XTD** plugins affect how your articles look when you're editing an article:

- **Editors** plugins provide the whole editor area at the top of your articles.

- **Editors-XTD** plugins provide extra features inside the editor area.

The image below shows only the Editors plugins:

The Editors plugins allow you to change the editor area for your articles. By default there are three options:

- Code Mirror: This provides a code editor for people who want to edit the article code directly.

- None: This provides a plain box with no editor.

- TinyMCE: This is the default editor that you've been looking at throughout the book.

It is possible to configure the editor options for your site.

- Go to "System", then "Global Configuration".

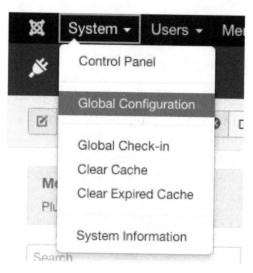

- Set "Default Editor" to "Code Mirror":

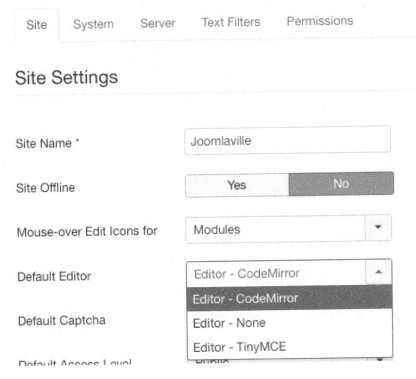

- Visit an article to see Code Mirror in action:

You can change the editor used on the site in two ways:

- **For everyone:** Go to the "System", then "Global Configuration", and change the "Default Editor" option.

- **For just one user:** Go to "Users", then "Manage". Click on the name of the user, click "Basic Settings", and you can change the "Editor" option for that single user:

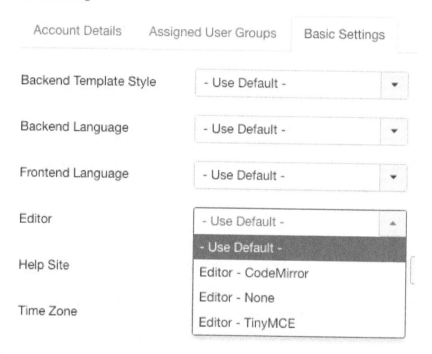

In addition to the Editors plugins, there are eight Editors-XTD plugins:

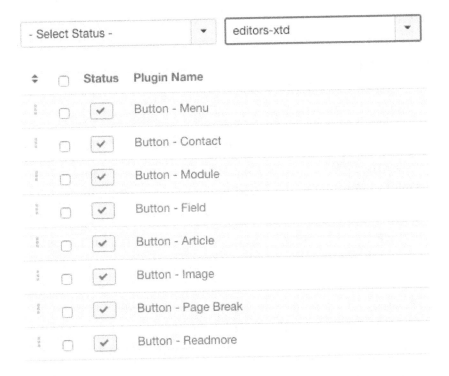

These buttons correspond directly to the buttons you see in your text editor: Module, Menu, Contact, Article, Image, Page Break and Read More.

## EXTENSION, SYSTEM, AND OTHER PLUGIN TYPES

There are several default plugin types that we haven't covered here, including the extension and system plugin types. You're unlikely to need to modify either of these beyond installing and enabling them, which is a process we cover in the next chapter.

- **Captcha:** These plugins can cut down on spam registrations or spam email via contact form by presenting a visual challenge that is easy for humans to identify but more difficult to spam software.

- **Extension:** These are tools used by developers to install and manage their extensions.
- **Fields:** Each of these plugins provides a different type of field.
- **Finder:** These plugins are for the Smart Search extension.
- **Installer:** These offer different ways to install extensions, as we'll see in the chapter "Adding Joomla Extensions Explained".
- **Quick icon:** These plugins allow developers to place images or messages on your dashboard when you first log in to your site's administrator area.
- **System:** These help your site operate smoothly. They can almost all be enabled and disabled from inside the Global Configuration screen. It's easier to manage them from there.
- **Twofactorauth:** These plugins add security to your site. We're going to cover these more in the chapter "Joomla Site Management Explained".
- **User:** These plugins add small extra features to user accounts.

WHAT'S NEXT?

Take a look at your site. You'll see that it has been barely altered during this chapter. Plugins work behind the scenes and don't create many visual changes.

After the last three chapters, you now understand how to manage the default extensions on your site. You know about components, modules, and also plugins.

But, what happens if you want more features than Joomla provides out-of-the-box? What happens if you want to add photo galleries, shopping carts, event calendars, social bookmarking links and more?

Let's turn the page and find out how to add extra features to Joomla.

# CHAPTER 12.

# ADDING JOOMLA EXTENSIONS EXPLAINED

It's time to move beyond the default extensions. We've shown you the components, modules, and plugins that you see when you install Joomla. In this chapter, we show you how to find extensions that meet the unique needs of your site.

After this chapter, you'll be able to research components, modules, and plugins. You'll also be able to install components, modules, and plugins.

## THE JOOMLA EXTENSIONS DIRECTORY

So far in this book, we've looked at the default components, modules, and plug-ins:

- **Components:** There were eleven, including Banners, Contacts, Redirects, and Search.

- **Modules:** There were more than twenty types of modules. We didn't look at every option, but we did practice with Search, Custom HTML, Articles – Latest, and more.

- **Plugins:** There were more than seventy types of plugins. We looked at some of them that allowed us to change our text editor, add voting on articles, and more.

Those default extensions are great for beginners. They serve as useful examples that you can use when learning Joomla. When it comes to building real sites, you'll probably have more advanced needs. You may already be thinking about photo galleries, videos, shopping carts, social networking and other features you'd like on your Joomla site.

There's one place to find all those features and more: http://extensions.joomla.org.

This site is known as the Joomla Extensions Directory (JED) and lists absolutely everything that you might want to add to your Joomla site. It is the key place to evaluate all the components, modules, and plugins you might want on your site. The JED is constantly being updated, improved, and looked after. Joomla users are always testing and providing feedback on the extensions. There are also JED administrators who are experienced Joomla people who monitor the extensions for problems. I wouldn't recommend going anywhere else to look for extensions. The following sections explain how we use it to find and evaluate extensions.

The JED is also available directly inside your site.

- Go to "Extensions", then "Manage". You'll see a message as shown on the screen below.

- Click the button labeled "Add 'Install from Web' tab".

- You should now see a page like the one in the image below:

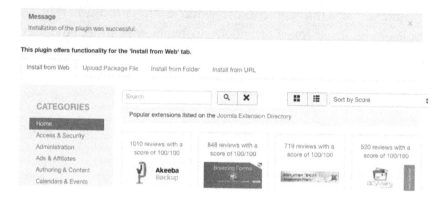

There are two ways to find what you're looking for here:

- There's a search box at the top of the page:

- There is a Categories list on the left sidebar:

## CATEGORIES

| |
|---|
| **Home** |
| Access & Security |
| Administration |
| Ads & Affiliates |
| Authoring & Content |
| Calendars & Events |
| Clients & Communities |
| Communication |
| Contacts & Feedback |
| Content Sharing |
| Core Enhancements |
| Directory & Documentation |
| e-Commerce |
| Editing |
| Extension Specific |
| Financial |

If you know what you're looking for and want to drill down quickly, then the Search box is a good option. When you're seeing the JED for the first time, the Categories list is good place to start. It allows us to browse if we're not sure exactly what we're looking for.

For example, let's see if we can find a good way to show videos on our site. Take a look down the list of categories and find a category that matches what you're looking for.

- Click on "Social Web". You'll see some sub-categories underneath:

- Click on "Social Media":

- You'll see a variety of video and media options:

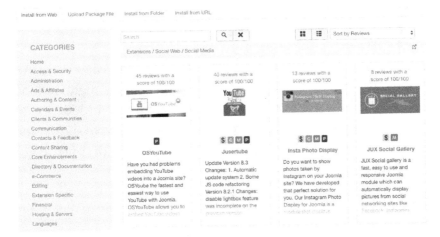

You definitely will not suffer from a lack of choice. As I write this there are thousands of extensions on the JED.

So what should you be looking for? Here are some important things that will help you find the right extension.

## Rating

The extensions show feedback from people like you. Joomla users are allowed to vote on extensions and leave their comments. The extensions that have the most positive feedback rise to the top. So, if we see many extensions in the Social Media category the quickest way to sort is by looking at the ratings. On the screen below you can see that all four extensions in the first row have a score of at least 100/100.

If you scroll to the bottom of the page, you'll see that there are many more of these extensions. Some extensions here have lower scores, meaning that users didn't have a very good experience. Some extensions might not have been used often enough to get many votes at all.

It's worth noting how many votes each extension has. An extension with 100/100 but only a few reviews might not be that good. An extension with no votes might be a hidden gem that is simply new or undiscovered. The image above shows one extension with forty-five reviews and one with only eight reviews.

## Cost

About 75% of the extensions on the JED are completely free to use. The other 25% of the extensions are commercial, and you have to pay to download them. They generally cost from $5 up to $100 for the most advanced.

In the image below, you can see that three extensions have $ symbols. Those extensions are commercial. Extensions without that dollar symbol are free.

Regardless of whether you use a free or commercial extension from the JED, they all have two things in common:

- You can use them on as many sites as you want.
- The code is completely open. If you know how, you can change anything and everything about how they work.

Remember that developing extensions is hard and everyone has bills to pay. Almost everyone who writes code for Joomla is able to do so because they make money from it in some way.

Free extension developers often make money by doing work for clients who need Joomla help. Even free extension developers have business models: after all, everyone needs to pay the bills and keep their lights on.

- Some use the extension as a form of advertising to help them attract business. For example, someone might download a photo gallery, realize that they need an extra feature, and then hire the developer of the photo gallery to code that feature.

- Some do work for clients and then get their permission to release the code afterwards.

- Some rely on donations. If you use a noncommercial extension and see a donation button on the developer's site, it's good practice to send them some money.

- Some may sell premium versions of their free extensions with more features and high priority support.

Commercial extension developers make money by selling their extensions. They have a variety of business models:

- Some charge for the extension. Often paying for the extension gives you access to download it and any updates for a certain period of time, such as six months or a year.

- Some provide the main part of the extension for free and charge for extra features.

- Some give the extension away for free and charge for support.

### Different Types of Extension

It's perfectly possible for one extra feature to require more than one kind of extension. Something can require a component, a module, and a plugin.

For example, Jusertube has the following extensions, as shown in the image below:

- C: a component

- M: a module

- P: a plugin

By looking also at the OSYoutube listing, we can work out three important pieces of information:

- **Rating:** 100/100, and 45 reviews

- **Free or commercial:** Free

- **Extension Types:** Plugin

Let's take a look at another extension. Insta Photo Display is also shown in the image above, and here's what we can tell about it:

- **Rating:** 100/100, and 13 reviews

- **Free or commercial:** Commercial

- **Extension Types:** Component, Module, and Plugin

Looking at all our options for videos, OSYouTube looks like a good place to start. It has very positive feedback and is free to download. Let's install OSYouTube and evaluate it further.

INSTALLING EXTENSIONS

Let's take you through the process of installing a new extension, using OSYouTube as an example:

- Click on the OSYouTube listing. You'll see a page like the one shown in the image below:

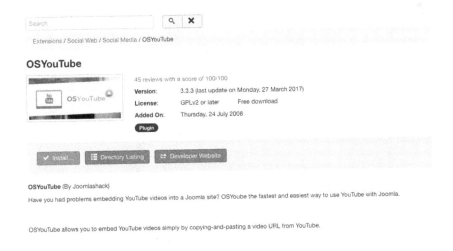

- Click the green "Install" button.

- You'll now be asked to confirm the installation. Click the blue "Install" button, as shown in the image below:

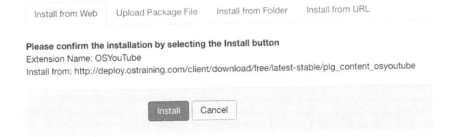

- You'll now see a message saying that the installation was successful. OSYouTube will also show some details, as in the image below. The description says, "With this plugin, you can embed YouTube videos into articles simply by copying and pasting a video URL from YouTube into an article".

With this plugin, you can embed YouTube videos into articles simply by copying and pasting a video URL from YouTube into an article with fluid responsive support.

**Thanks for installing OSYouTube!**

Show more details...

✔ Go Pro to access more features

Like this extension? Leave a review on the JED ★ ★ ★ ★ ★

Powered by **Joomlashack**

© 2017 Joomlashack.com. All rights reserved

- Let's follow the instructions in the plugin description.

- Go to YouTube.com and get the URL of a video. The URL will look like this: https://www.youtube.com/watch?v=XpBGeHkfXpc

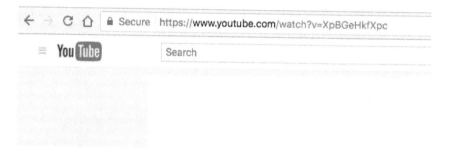

- In your Joomla site, go to "Content" and "Articles".

- Open the "About Joomlaville" article.

- Paste the URL into the bottom of the article:

Who Lives in Joomlaville?

Joomlaville is full of people who love Joomla! Find out more at the official Joomla website.

What Are People Looking for in Joomlaville?

These are some popular articles on our site:

{loadmodule mod_articles_popular,Popular Articles}

https://www.youtube.com/watch?v=XpBGeHkfXpc

- Save the article and visit the front of your site. You will see your video is playing on the homepage:

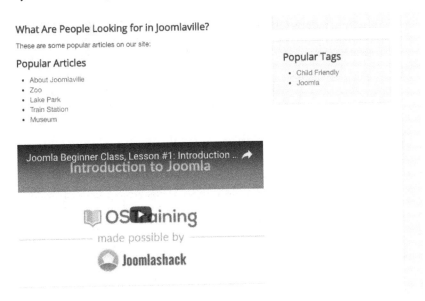

All in all, OSYouTube seems to be a reliable extension that does what we need: it allows us to easily show videos.

In this example, the developers of OSYouTube pay their bills by developing a premium version of OSYouTube with more features. "OSYouTube Pro" is available at https://joomlashack.com/joomla-extensions/osyoutube/.

That's how we find and evaluate an extension. You could repeat the same process on any other kind of extension you want on your site, and you practice this later in the chapter.

- Research: We use the extension search to evaluate extensions.
- Install: We install the extension and test it to see if it meets our needs.

This process will work for a majority of extensions. We're going to practice that process several more times in the next part of this chapter.

Some extensions may require a slightly different process (such as opening your wallet, in 25% of cases!), but they are all similar.

## INSTALLING A SOCIAL BOOKMARKING EXTENSION

In our next example, we're going to show social bookmarking links on our articles.

- Go to "Extensions", then "Install".
- Click the "Social Web" category, then the "Social Share" category.

- You'll now see a list of extensions, as shown in the image below:

Let's recap what we're looking for:

- **Features:** Show social bookmarks on articles
- **Rating:** The best we can find
- **Free or commercial:** Free

Many of these extensions have very positive feedback, but we can eliminate the first two because they have Commercial icons. That leaves us with Social 2s or CoalaWeb Social Links. It's not an easy decision, because they're equal in almost every aspect. However, I'm going to lean towards testing Social2s first, because it looks like a simpler alternative. Social2s just has a plugin, whereas CoalaWebSocial Links has a Component, Module, and Plugin.

- Click on Social2s
- Click "Install".
- Click "Install" again to confirm the installation.

Now we can go and enable the plugin.

- Go to Extensions, then "Plugins".
- Search for "social":

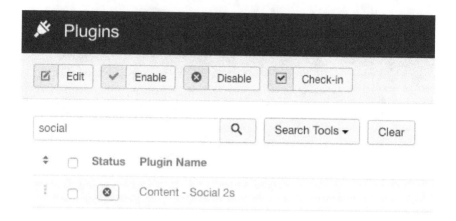

- Click the red button so that it turns to a green check mark. This will enable the plugin.

- Visit the front of your site and check that the social bookmarks have appeared. You'll find them at the bottom of articles:

powered by social2s

- The plugin seems to work well. If I click the Twitter button, I see a pop-up window asking me to tweet:

All-in-all this plugin seems reliable, but there are some changes to be made. For example, the extension includes a link back to the author. We should remove that.

- In your Joomla admin, go back to "Extensions", then "Plugins".
- Edit the Social 2s plugin.
- Under the "License" tab, there's an option to disable the link:

- There are also several other tabs with customization options. For example, you can change the social networks, or choose to have the social links only appear on some articles.

As with OSYouTube, you can see that the developer provides a great extension for free, but they also have a business model. You can buy a Pro version of the extension with more features.

### Installing a Sitemap Extension

The third example we're going to use is a sitemap extension. We're going to find an extension that will allow us to show a sitemap for our content.

- Go to Extensions, then "Install".
- Search for "sitemap" using the search box:

Popular extensions listed on the Joomla Extension Directory

In this case, the results are more complex than with video or social bookmarking extensions. Let's recap what we're looking for:

- **Features:** Show a sitemap
- **Rating:** The best we can find
- **Free or commercial:** Free

However, the results mostly show commercial listings, or extensions that don't seem to be what we need. JSitemap, obRSS and Ping Search Engines are all commercial. EKS has a confusing description that doesn't seem relevant.

As we scroll down through the results, almost all the extensions are either commercial or have little feedback. It's not until we get down to these listings that we see some progress. OSMap is free and popular (92 reviews). Although it's overall score is not 100/100, it's score of 74 is not terrible.

- 92 reviews with a score of 74/100 — **OSMap** — OSMap is the best and easiest Joomla sitemap. OSMap will help Google and other search engines understand your site content. Anything you can do to help Google read your site is a good thing. This is why we develop OSMap. OSMap is the easiest way

- 5 reviews with a score of 74/100 — **Route 66** — Beautiful SEF URLs, Facebook Instant Articles and XML Sitemaps for your Joomla! site! ###Flexible SEF URLs definition using patterns Route 66 allows you to define your site SEF URLs using patterns and not be restricted by limited URL

- 2 reviews with a score of 73/100 — **Sitemap Cache** — You might not know that using such popular extensions, as OSMap, XMap, MapX without caching can down your server completely. It is easy to make your site unresponsive by doing a school DDOS (HTTP flood) attack

- 1 reviews with a score of 73/100 — **google Sitemap for virtuemart** — Easy add your ''products and categories sitemap'' in Google webmastertools with this component. ###Setting Free Go to your ''virtuemart 2+ SiteMap'' component, all your virtuemart language are displayed and you

- Click "OSMap".

- Click "Install", and then "Install" again.

- Go to "Components", then "OSMap Free".

- You'll see that a sitemap has been created for you:

- The XML option is a technical version for Google. The human-readable version is marked as HTML. Click on that "HTML" link, and you'll see a sitemap like this:

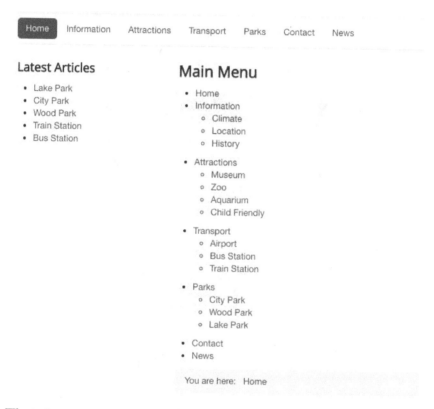

That sitemap seems to work well, so let's add it to a menu for our visitors to see:

- Go to "Menus", "Main Menu", then "Add New Menu Item"
- Menu Title: **Sitemap**
- Menu Item Type: **Sitemap – HTML Format**

- Choose a sitemap: **Default Sitemap**
- Save the menu link and visit the front of your site. You'll see the sitemap is visible:

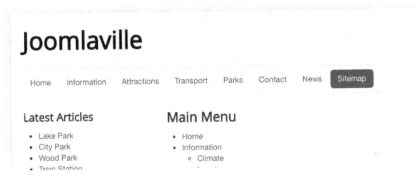

There's only one thing that really needs to be changed here. The sitemap is showing the menu title: Main Menu. To disable this, edit the menu link. Under the "Sitemap Settings" tab, you can set "Show Menu Titles" to "No":

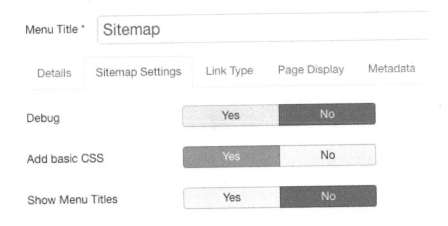

## OTHER INSTALLATION METHODS

It's wonderful that so many extensions can be installed so easily. However, not all extensions can be installed this way. There are two common exceptions:

- Extensions that require you to visit the developer's website to download the files.

- Commercial extensions.

If someone does provide you with an extension like this, it will be in a .zip file. Don't worry, it's easy to install. We have an example file available for you at http://ostra.in/osmeta. This extension is called OSMeta and will improve your metadata for search engines.

- Click the http://ostra.in/osmeta link, and you'll get a file downloaded to your desktop. The name of the file will look like com_osmeta_free_1.4.5.zip.

- In your Joomla site, go to "Extensions", then "Install".

- Click the "Upload Package File" tab.

- Drag-and-drop the zip file from your desktop into the upload area. That's it! The extension will upload successfully.

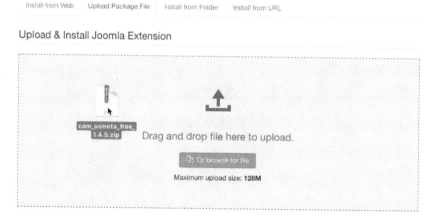

Install from Web    Upload Package File    Install from Folder    Install from URL

Upload & Install Joomla Extension

com_osmeta_free_
1.4.5.zip    Drag and drop file here to upload.

Or browse for file

Maximum upload size: **128M**

- To use this new extension, go to "Components", then "OSMeta Free".

- On a single screen, you'll be able to update the search engine title and description for all your articles:

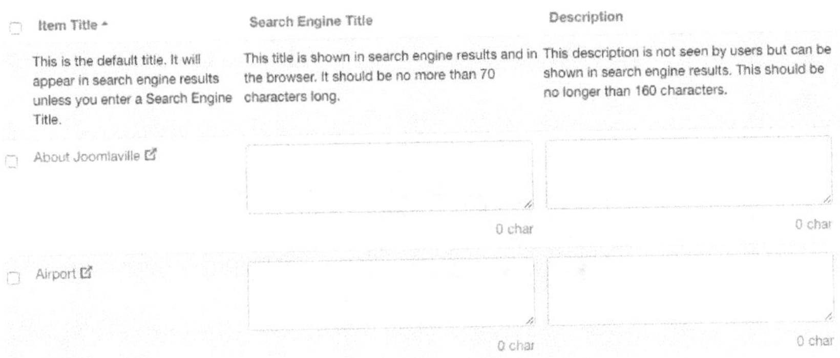
Item Title
Search Engine Title
Description
This is the default title. It will appear in search engine results unless you enter a Search Engine Title.
This title is shown in search engine results and in the browser. It should be no more than 70 characters long.
This description is not seen by users but can be shown in search engine results. This should be no longer than 160 characters.
About Joomlaville
0 char
0 char
Airport
0 char
0 char

These titles and descriptions are not visible on the page, but they will appear in Google's search results. Here's an example from the OSTraining site:

- Title: The OSTraining Blog – Web Design News and Tutorials
- Description: The OSTraining blog features news and tutorials about WordPress, Drupal, Joomla and other major open source platforms.

The OSTraining Blog - Web Design News and Tutorials
https://www.ostraining.com/blog/
May 11, 2017 - The OSTraining blog features news and tutorials about WordPress, Drupal, Joomla and other major open source platforms.

We've installed multiple extensions during this chapter, and our site has several new features. We can now add videos and social bookmarks to our content. We can also optimize our site for search engines with a sitemap, and the ability to update the search engine title and description.

Now that you're at the end of this chapter, your Joomlaville site should look similar to the image below:

# Joomlaville

Search ...

**Home** | Information | Attractions | Transport | Parks | Contact | News | Sitemap

**Latest Articles**
- Lake Park
- City Park
- Wood Park
- Train Station
- Bus Station

**Popular Articles**
- About Joomlaville
- Zoo
- Lake Park
- Train Station
- Museum

## About Joomlaville

Joomla

**Thank you for visiting our site for the city of Joomlaville.**

It's a *wonderful city* to live in, and we hope you'll visit us soon. The weather is beautiful in the summer and not too cold in the winter, so it is always a good time to visit.

### Joomlaville Visitor Suggestions

Joomlaville has lots to do. Here are some suggestions if you are new to Joomlaville.

You can visit:

- the Aquarium
- the Zoo
- the Museum

You can get here via the Airport, Bus Station and Train Station.

### Who Lives in Joomlaville?

Joomlaville is full of people who love Joomla! Find out more at the official Joomla website.

### What Are People Looking for in Joomlaville?

These are some popular articles on our site:

**Popular Articles**
- About Joomlaville
- Zoo
- Lake Park
- Train Station
- Museum

**Joomlaville Information**

History
Location
Climate

SUPPORT

Joomla!

**Login Form**

| Username |
| Password |
Remember Me
Log in

Forgot your username?
Forgot your password?

**Popular Tags**
- Child Friendly
- Joomla

Joomla Beginner Class, Lesson #1: Introduction ...
Introduction to Joomla

OS Training

made possible by

Joomlashack

You are here:  Home

## WHAT'S NEXT?

You now know how to add the features you need to build a Joomla site.

Our next step will be design. In Joomla, we use templates to control our site's design.

We're going to use templates to improve the design, the color scheme and the layout of our site.

Turn the page, and let's talk about Joomla templates.

# CHAPTER 13.

## JOOMLA TEMPLATES EXPLAINED

Templates control the design and layout of your Joomla site.

- If you want a pink and green site, look for a pink and green template.
- If you want a site with a large header banner, look for a template with room for it.
- If you want to build a business site, look for a template with a corporate look and feel.
- If you want to build a personal blog, look for a template that reflects your personality.

Joomla arrives with three default templates for your site's visitors, and in this chapter we show you how they work. We'll also show you how to find and add extra templates that have more features and a wider variety of designs.

### UNDERSTANDING TEMPLATES

Templates are what attract many people to Joomla. You can use an amazing variety of designs and possibilities. With just a few clicks of your mouse, you can completely redesign your site.

The image below shows Mondrian from Joomlashack. Mondrian is focused on event websites.

The image below shows a template called Joline from a company called YooTheme. This template is designed for health and wellness websites:

The image below shows a more corporate design. This template is called Topaz and is developed by a company called Rocketheme.

No matter what type of site you want to build, you can find a template to meet your needs.

Before we show you how they work, here is one important thing to know about templates: They do not change your content in any way.

If you change your template, your articles stay the same. If you change your template, your components stay the same. They may look different, but their content will not change. If you publish a template that you don't like, you can just revert back to the previous template, and everything will be back to the way it was before.

## CHANGING TEMPLATES

By default, two templates are installed on your Joomla site.

- Go to "Extensions" and then "Templates":

There are two options: Beez3 and Protostar. Notice that little gold star next to Protostar? That means it's the default template. We've been using it throughout the book.

Let's take a look at Beez3, the other template. Beez3 was the default template in previous versions of Joomla, but has been replaced by Protostar.

- In the "Default" column, click on the star in the Beez3 row":

- Go to the front of your site to see the new design, as in the image below:

All our content is still there, but there also some significant differences:

- The content in modules is still showing, but has moved around.
- This template doesn't support dropdown menus, so the Main Menu is broken.
- The site's color scheme has changed.

So in the default Joomla installation, Beez3 is the only alternative to Protostar. However, there are some changes we can make to both of these templates. Let's look at template options.

## CHANGING TEMPLATE OPTIONS

We can redesign our site by changing the template. However, it's also possible to redesign our site and still keep the same template. Most templates come with design options.

Let's use Protostar as an example and make it into the default template again:

- Go to "Extensions", then "Templates".
- Look for the Default column and click on the star in the Protostar row.
- Click on the "protostar – Default" name.
- Click the "Advanced" tab. You'll now see several options for changing the Protostar design:

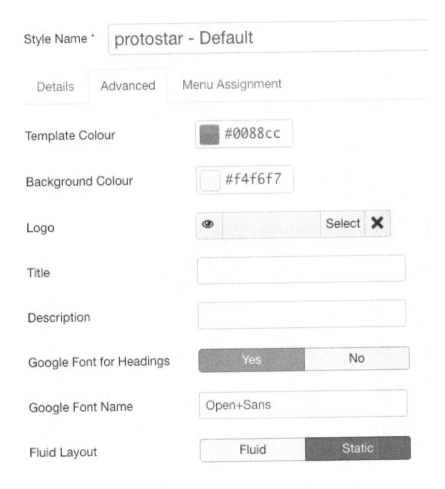

- Click the "Template Colour" box, and you'll get a pop-up. You can use this to select a new color scheme for the site.

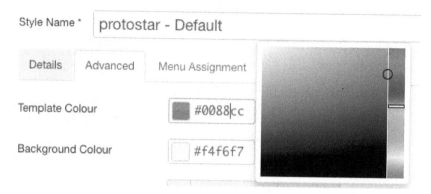

- Choose a different color for the "Template Colour" option.

- Choose a different color for the "Background Colour" option.

- Save the template, and view your site. You should now see that your site looks very different. I decided to make my template pink and green:

Each template has different options. Some allow you to change the design. Some allow you to change the layout. Some have no options at all.

- Go to "Extensions, then "Templates".

- Click the "Beez3" name and then the "Advanced" tab. You'll now see a screen like the one below. These are the options for the Beez3 template.

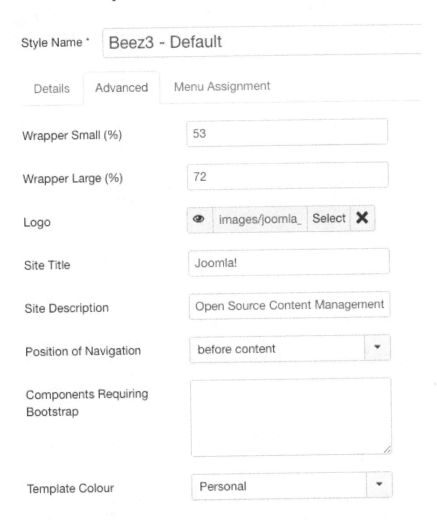

Some of the design options for templates can become advanced. The template shown below is the a template from Rockettheme, who we introduced earlier. This template provides pages and pages full of options.

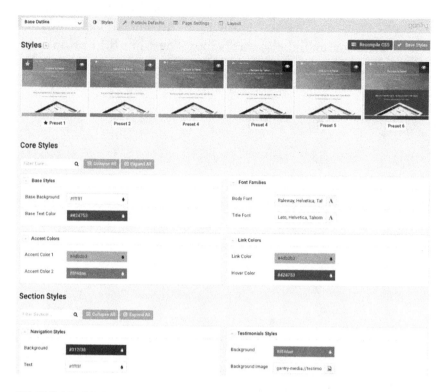

## FINDING AND INSTALLING TEMPLATES

So if we want to change our site's design or layout, we have two options:

- We can change the template.
- If our existing template has the appropriate options, we can change those.

We are starting with only two existing templates (Protostar or Beez3), so unless we want to use those, we will need to find and install a new template. There are at least two important differences between extensions and templates:

- **Directory:** There is no equivalent of the Joomla Extensions Directory for templates. What that means is the templates generally can't be evaluated so easily. Evaluation is mostly done by viewing a template demo or actually installing and testing the template. Unlike components, modules, and plug-ins, it's harder to find unbiased information, ratings, and reviews to rely on.

- **Price:** Whereas 75% of components, modules, and plug-ins are noncommercial, the opposite is true with templates. The majority of templates are sold by commercial companies. However, competition is strong between these companies, and that keeps prices low. Prices for single templates generally range from $10 up to around $50. Many companies also run template clubs where you can buy a subscription to download all their templates for a limited period of time. For example, at Joomlashack you pay $65 and get access to all their templates for 6 months.

## FINDING A TEMPLATE

Here are the criteria I recommend beginners to use when finding a template. Most of them are the same as for components, modules, and plug-ins:

- **Commercial or Non-Commercial:** Do you want to pay?

- **Documentation:** How well documented is it?

- **Support:** Is there ongoing support for the template?

- **Design:** This is specific only to templates. Does it match the look and the feel that you want for your site? Especially when you're getting started, you have enough to worry about without digging into the code of templates and working hard to make it look the way you want. It's better to start with a template that's as close as possible to the end result that you want.

Let's start with a template from Joomlashack called "Community". This is a normally a commercial template, but they've made it free for readers of this book.

You can download Community here: http://ostra.in/downloadcommunity

- Download Community to your desktop.

- Go to your Joomla site. Go to "Extensions", "Manage", and then "Install".

- Drag-and-drop the Community file into the upload area:

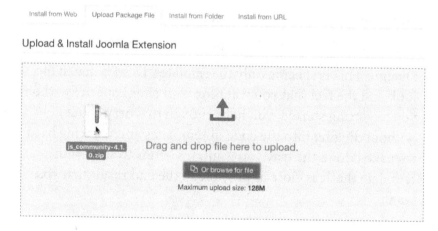

- You should you see a success message:

# C•mmunity

This is the js_community template by Joomlashack
v.4.1.0

Thanks for installing the js_community template. Now you can go to the Template Manager to configure it.

- Go to "Extensions", then "Templates".

- Make Community into the default template.

- Visit the front of your site, and you'll see the new template in action. We clearly have some more work to do:

## C•mmunity

About Joomlaville

 Joomla

Thank you for visiting our site for the city of Joomlaville.

It's a *wonderful city* to live in, and we hope you'll visit us soon. The weather is beautiful in the summer and not too cold in the winter, so it is always a good time to visit.

### Joomlaville Visitor Suggestions

Joomlaville has lots to do. Here are some suggestions if you are new to Joomlaville.

You can visit:

- the Aquarium
- the Zoo
- the Museum

You can get here via the Airport, Bus Station and Train Station.

### Who Lives in Joomlaville?

Joomlaville is full of people who love Joomla! Find out more at the official Joomla website.

### What Are People Looking for in Joomlaville?

These are some popular articles on our site:

The left and right sidebars have disappeared. What happened to those modules in the sidebars?

Think back to when we were working with modules. We went to the "Templates" screen and clicked Preview next to the Protostar template. The image below shows the module positions we saw:

Let's compare this to the documentation on the Joomlashack site, which shows the module positions for Community: https://joomlashack.com/joomla-templates/community-social-easy/.

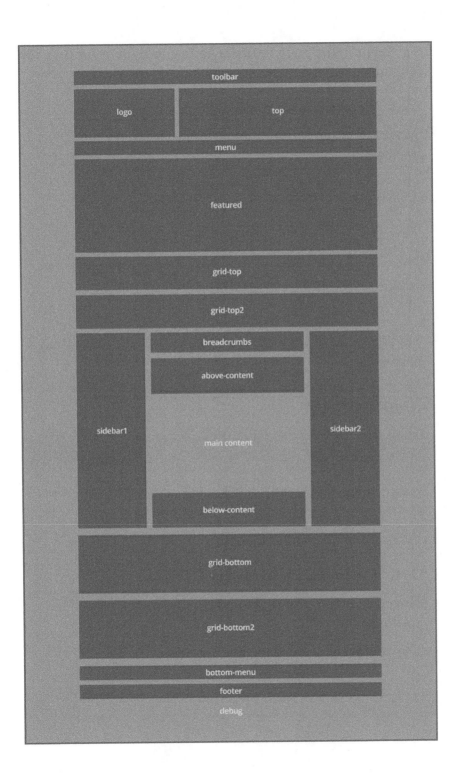

Let's start to adapt our modules to match the positions in the Community template. Let's start with the Main Menu.

- Go to "Extensions", then "Modules".
- Move the "Main Menu" module to the "Menu [menu]" position:

- Visit the front of your site, and the menu should be working correctly:

Let's try that with another module:

- Go to "Extensions", then "Modules".
- Move the "Smart Search" module to the "Menu [menu]" position.
- This is how the search box now appears:

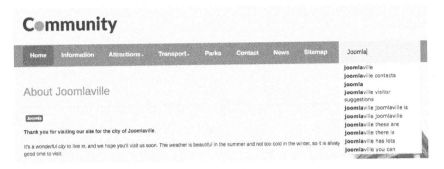

That looks great, but there are a couple of small improvements we can make.

First, take a close look at the Community demo: https://community4.joomlatemplate.joomlashack.com. You'll notice that the search box has a small icon in the corner:

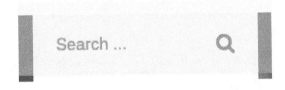

This redesigning of modules can be done with with a feature called module class suffixes. You can see some examples for Community at https://community4.joomlatemplate.joomlashack.com/documentation/module-styles-and-positions. These suffixes are different for each template.

Here's how it works for the Community template and our search box:

- On the "Modules" screen, edit the "Smart Search" module.
- Click the "Advanced" tab.
- In the "Module Class Suffix field, enter " pull-right". Yes, you do need that space.

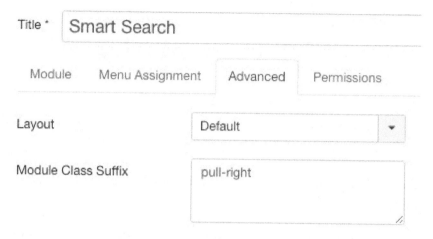

Title *  Smart Search

Module    Menu Assignment    Advanced    Permissions

Layout                          Default                      ▼

Module Class Suffix             pull-right

- Save the Smart Search module and your search box will have the magnifying glass icon too.

Next, we can put the login module on the homepage. This will match the demo.

- On the "Modules" screen, edit the "Login Form" module.
- Show Title: **Hide**
- Position: **Featured**
- Module Assignment: **Only on the pages selected**
- Menu Selection: **Home**

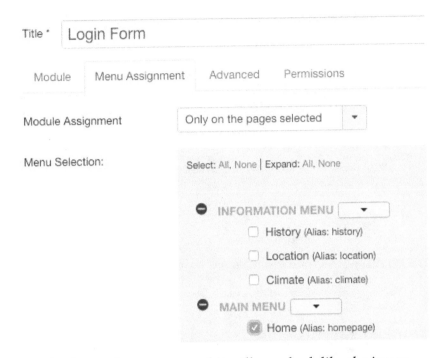

- Refresh your homepage, and it will now look like the image below. That's pretty good progress!

Let's click through the menu links to see how things look.

Generally, the pages look good, but there are some things to fix:

- There's still no sidebar content.
- The social bookmarking plugin doesn't look good:

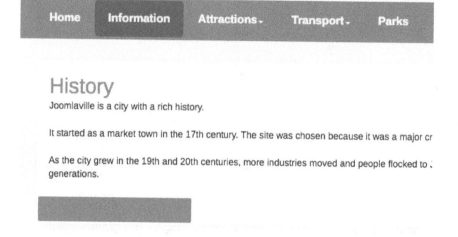

First, let's bring our sidebar modules back.

- Go to "Extensions", then "Modules".
- Select all the modules that had been in your sidebars:

- Click the "Batch" button in the toolbar:

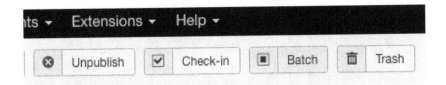

- Choose "Sidebar2 [sidebar2]" for the position.
- Click "Process".

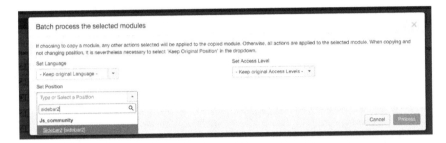

- All your sidebar modules are now back in the sidebar:

Search ... Q

## Latest Articles

- Lake Park
- City Park
- Wood Park
- Train Station
- Bus Station

## Popular Articles

- About Joomlaville
- Zoo
- Lake Park
- Train Station
- Museum

## Joomlaville Information

History

Location

Climate

—— SUPPORT ——

Next, let's fix the social bookmarking links.

- Go to "Extensions", then "Plugins" and edit the Social2S plugin.
- Under the "Article" dropdown, change the "Style" to "icon_colour".

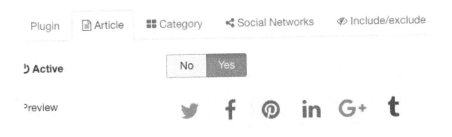

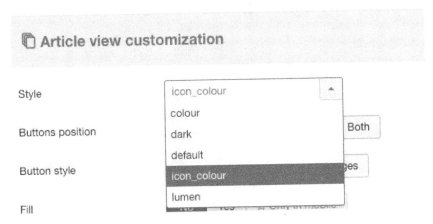

- Visit your site and the icons will now look much better:

We only have one thing left to do now, which is to add our own logo and homepage image.

- Go to https://ostraining.com/books/j3e/chapter12/ and download the logo.
- In your Joomla site, go to "Content" and then "Media".
- Upload the logo file into the main folder of your media gallery.
- Go to "Extensions", then "Templates" and edit the Community template.
- Choose your newly uploaded logo file from the "Logo Image" dropdown:

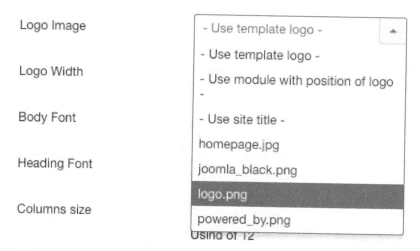

- Visit your homepage, and there's your logo:

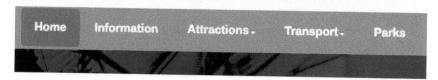

Now let's move onto the homepage image.

- Still editing the Community options, click the "Community Options" tab.

- Select a new image for your "Default Featured image". I choose the homepage.jpg image that we uploaded earlier in the book.

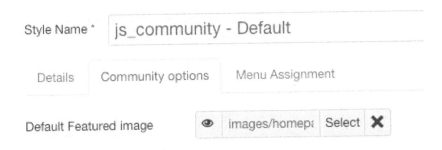

- Visit your homepage, and there's your new image:

I can't promise that every template is as good or easy-to-use as Community, but that has ended up with a great end-result for our site.

In addition to choosing a good template for you, I did also provide unusually clear guidelines on how to set it up. When you come to choose a good template, you will need to rely on documentation from the designer.

## AN OVERVIEW OF TEMPLATES

It's obviously unfair of me to pick a few example templates (Joomlashack, YooTheme and Rockettheme) out of the hundreds of template companies. However, as a Joomla beginner you need to start somewhere, and these three give an interesting introduction to the variety of designs you can pick from.

Notice a few things looking at these sites:

- **Each template company has a very different style.** Most of these companies have 50 or more templates on offer, but each one has a style: colorful or minimal, corporate or fun, busy or plain. Pick the style that meets the needs of your site.

- **Prices:** Most companies sell download access to multiple templates for a fixed period of time. Some companies sell individual templates, but the majority are time-based. You can use the templates forever, but only download them for that fixed period of time.

- **Complexity:** Be warned! Some of these templates can get pretty complicated. Don't imagine that your template will look as good as the demos as soon as you upload them. The demo sites have been set up by experts. Some template companies solve that problem by providing copies of Joomla that come prepackaged with their template and any needed extensions already set up correctly. Instead of downloading Joomla from http://joomla.org, you would download and install their copy of Joomla.

After all the design work we've done, here's what our site looks like at the end of this chapter:

## WHAT'S NEXT?

We now have a site that looks much better.

We are almost ready to start letting people use our site. We need to think about our users.

If we have people registering on our site, we need to control what content and extensions we show them.

Turn the page, and we're going to talk about user management in Joomla.

# CHAPTER 14.

## JOOMLA USERS EXPLAINED

Up until this part of the book, you learned almost everything that is essential to know about Joomla.

We have seen nearly all areas of the Joomla administrator area, but you probably noticed that we have skipped over one area: Users. That area is the focus of this chapter.

After reading this chapter, you'll be able to do the following:

- Understand Joomla's three default access levels that control what people see on your site
- Understand Joomla's eight default user groups that control what people can do on your site
- Modify those access levels and user groups to meet the unique needs of your site

### THREE DIFFERENT APPROACHES TO USER MANAGEMENT

Imagine that you have launched your Joomlaville site. You have many different types of visitors. Here are some fairly simple examples:

- **The public:** They're just curious and want to browse around your site.

- **Registered users:** They want to log in and submit news articles and events.

- **Administrators:** They want to add content, move modules, add menu links, and do whatever else they need to manage the site.

Each of these types of visitors needs different permissions for different areas of the site. For example, we don't want to allow the general public to submit articles because we'd get too much spam.

How do we give different permissions to different types of visitors? That's the question we're going to answer in this chapter.

We recommend three different ways to approach user management:

- **Method 1:** Access Levels. This involves using Joomla's default setup to control what people can see.

- **Method 2:** Using Joomla's default setup to control what people can do.

- **Method 3:** Modifying Joomla's default setup to create your own lists of what people can see and do. This is the most complex way of handling users.

User management can quickly become complex. I recommend that you always choose the simplest setup you can think of.

## METHOD 1: ACCESS LEVELS

First, let's see how we can control what our site visitors can and cannot access on your site.

- Go to "Content, then "Articles".

- You can see all of the articles that you have added in the previous chapters, as shown in the image below. Notice that there's a column called Access that we haven't mentioned yet. Every article has the same entry: Public. That means that these articles are all available to the general public. Any visitor to our site can access every one of these articles.

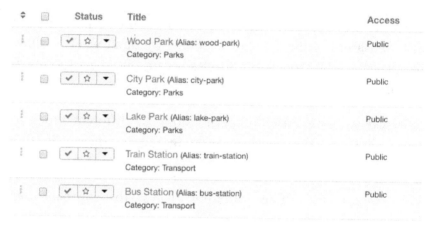

- Click on the City Park article.
- You'll now see the same article editing screen that we used so often throughout the book. You can see there's an "Access" field here too. Click on that "Access" field, and a dropdown menu appears, as in the image below:

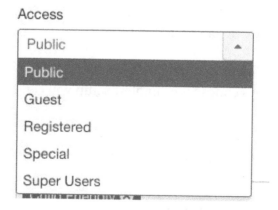

Public is the default choice, but there are four other options:

Guest, Registered, Special, and Super Users. Here's what the choices mean:

- **Public:** Accessible to everyone
- **Guest:** Accessible only to users who are not logged in
- **Registered:** Accessible only to people who create an account and log in
- **Special:** Accessible only to the users who will maintain the site. This covers everyone from Authors, who can only write content, all the way up to Super Users, who can control everything on the site.
- **Super Users:** Accessible only to the most powerful users on the site

Let's see how those options work in practice:

- Select "Registered" as the choice for the "Access" dropdown and click "Save & Close".
- Go to the visitor area of your site. See if you can find that City Park article you just saved. You can try the search box. You can try clicking on "Parks" in the menu. You can look all around the site, but you won't find the article.
- Now, look for the Login Form module on the homepage. Log in here using the same username and password that you use for the administrator area.
- After you've logged in successfully, you can see that the Login Form module has changed. The module no longer shows the information that the general public needs, such as how to register or recover a forgotten password. Now it just shows you a welcome message and a "Log out" button.

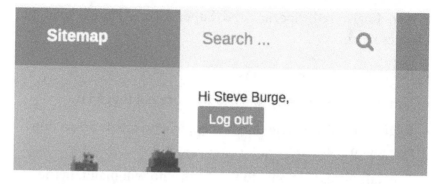

- Click the "Parks" menu link, and you should now be able to see the City Park article.

- Notice also that the "User Menu" has reappeared. None of those are links that would be either useful or safe to present to the general public.

# User Menu

Your Profile

Submit an Article

Site Administrator

Template Settings

Site Settings

- You can also see a cog icon next to each article, as shown in the image below. This allows you to edit the article directly from here.

n the

- This next image shows how you can edit an article via the frontend of your site. You have access to this editing screen pencil because you are a Super User. The cog didn't show before you logged in, because we definitely don't want to allow any ordinary members of the public to do this. From here you can edit the text and change a variety of options for the article, including the category, publishing dates, and more.

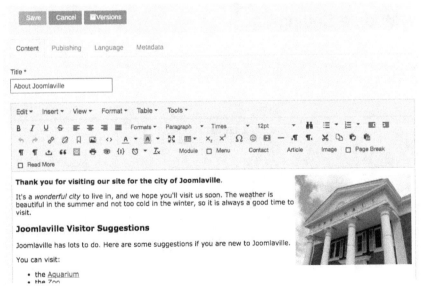

- Your site's modules will also have edit links:

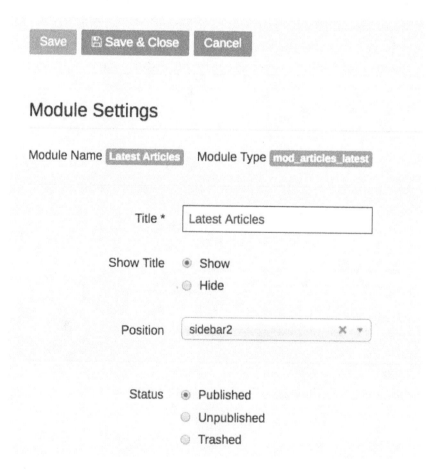

- You can edit the module settings from the frontend of your site:

That's the concept behind access levels: You can give different access permissions to different people on your site. The public sees one version of the site, and people at the different access levels see different versions of the site. Let's see how far this goes by looking at the administrator area again:

- Go back to the administrator area. Go to the Main Menu. You can see that Access is an option for all of your menu links, as shown below:

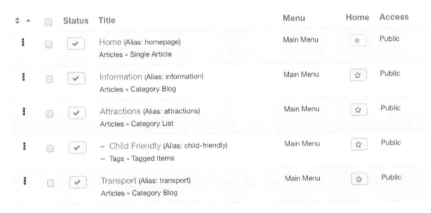

- Now go to your modules. You can see that Access is an option for all of your modules, as shown below:

You can keep on moving through your administrator area, but you see the same Access option almost everywhere you go. This means that you can control who sees what for most of the features on your site, from articles to menu links to modules.

Let's try another example. Remember the five definitions we gave earlier? Here they are again:

- **Guest:** Accessible only to users who are not logged in
- **Public:** Accessible to everyone
- **Super Users:** Accessible to only the most powerful users on the site
- **Registered:** Accessible only to people who create an account and log in
- **Special:** Accessible only to the users who will maintain the site. This covers everyone from Authors, who can only write content, all the way up to Super Users, who can control everything on the site.

Let's try an example at the Registered level. Here's how we're going to do it:

- On the Modules screen, click on the "Popular Articles" module.
- Change the "Access" option to "Registered".
- Click "Save & Close".
- Visit the front of your site and click on "Log out" inside the homepage Login Form. Notice that the "Popular Articles" module is no longer visible. You are just "Public" and are no longer counted as "Registered".

Now we're going to create a new user account so you can see how that works. By default, Joomla doesn't allow random people to create new accounts (this is done to prevent spam registrations), so we'll need to enable the feature.

- In your administrator area, go to "Users", "Manage", and click the "Options" button.
- Set "Allow User Registration" to "Yes".

- Set "New User Account Activation" to "None". This will avoid any moderation of new accounts.

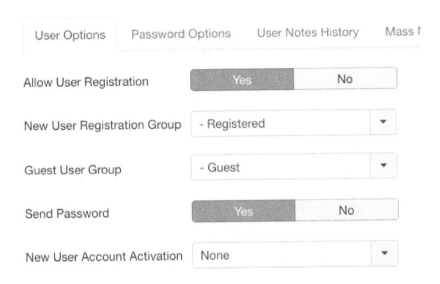

- Go back to the front of your site, and you'll now see a "Create an account" link:

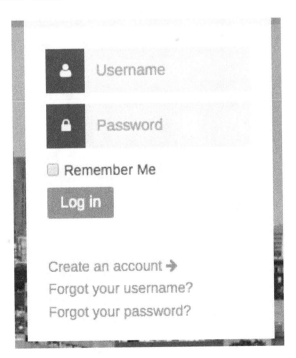

- Enter the details that Joomla needs. I'm going to use **registereduser** for all the fields except email. I will use a valid email address.

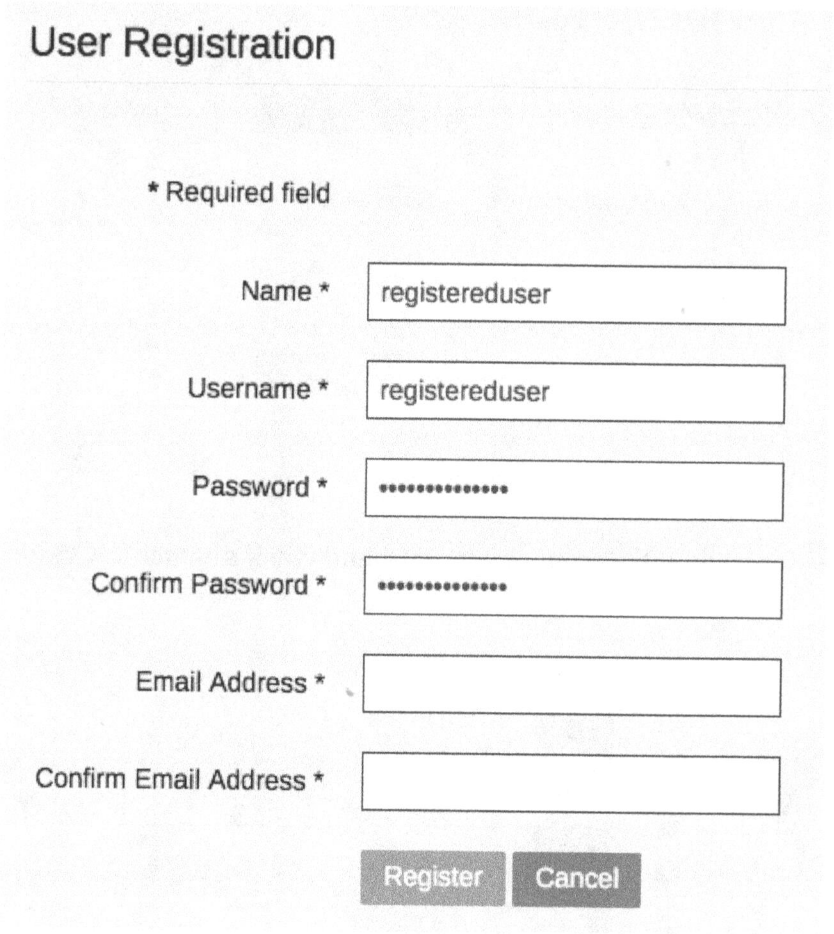

## User Registration

* Required field

| | |
|---|---|
| Name * | registereduser |
| Username * | registereduser |
| Password * | •••••••••••••• |
| Confirm Password * | •••••••••••••• |
| Email Address * | |
| Confirm Email Address * | |

Register  Cancel

- You now get a message saying, "Thank you for registering. You may now log in using the username and password you registered with." Go ahead and login:

Username *

Password *

Remember me

Log in

- You'll be taken immediately to your user profile page:

Profile                                                                      Edit Profile

| | |
|---|---|
| Name | registereduser |
| Username | registereduser |
| Registered Date | Thursday, 25 May 2017 |
| Last Visited Date | Thursday, 25 May 2017 |

This new user's account has been automatically created at the Registered level. Don't worry about people at this Registered level. They have a very safe set of permissions. Try browsing around the site. You'll see that you really don't have the ability to do much that a Public user could not.

For example, try to log in to the administrator area using your new account. You get a message saying you don't have permission, like the one you see below. Why were you denied access? It's because users can only access the administrator area if they have one of the highest permission levels. This is a security feature, and you should think carefully about who you allow to access the administrator area.

So the very basic way to control Joomla users is with the five basic user levels:

- **Guest:** Accessible only to users who are not logged in
- **Public:** Accessible to everyone
- **Super Users:** Accessible to only the most powerful users on the site
- **Registered:** Accessible only to people who create an account and log in
- **Special:** Accessible only to the users who will maintain the site. This covers everyone from Authors, who can only write content, all the way up to Super Users, who can control everything on the site.

You can see these five access levels if you go to "Users", then "Access Levels". Your screen will look like the one below:

| | | | Level Name | User Groups Having Viewing Access |
|---|---|---|---|---|
| ⇕ | ▲ | ☐ | | |
| ⋮ | | ☐ | Public | Public |
| ⋮ | | ☐ | Guest | Guest |
| ⋮ | | ☐ | Registered | Manager, Registered, Super Users |
| ⋮ | | ☐ | Special | Author, Manager, Super Users |
| ⋮ | | ☐ | Super Users | Super Users |

## METHOD 2: USER GROUPS

The five access levels work great for many sites. However, for some sites you want to do more than control what users can access: You also want to control what users can do.

Joomla comes with eight examples of user groups. There are Public and Registered, which correspond directly to the Public and Registered access levels that we just saw. The added examples are inside the Special access level. These groups are Author, Editor, Publisher, Manager, Administrator, and Super User.

Here is a chart of these groups and what they can and cannot do:

| Joomla 3 Permission table | | User groups | | | | | | | |
|---|---|---|---|---|---|---|---|---|---|
| | | Unregistered | Registered | Author | Editor | Publisher | Manager | Administrator | Super Administrator |
| View "public" | | ✓ | ✓ | ✓ | ✓ | ✓ | ✓ | ✓ | ✓ |
| View "registered" | | ✗ | ✓ | ✓ | ✓ | ✓ | ✓ | ✓ | ✓ |
| View "special" | | ✗ | ✗ | ✓ | ✓ | ✓ | ✓ | ✓ | ✓ |
| Create | Content | ✗ | ✗ | ✓ | ✓ | ✓ | ✓ | ✓ | ✓ |
| Edit own | | ✗ | ✗ | ✓ | ✓ | ✓ | ✓ | ✓ | ✓ |
| Edit all | | ✗ | ✗ | ✗ | ✓ | ✓ | ✓ | ✓ | ✓ |
| Publish new | | ✗ | ✗ | ✗ | ✗ | ✓ | ✓ | ✓ | ✓ |
| Access the administrator area | | ✗ | ✗ | ✗ | ✗ | ✗ | ✓ | ✓ | ✓ |
| Manage users | | ✗ | ✗ | ✗ | ✗ | ✗ | ✗ | ✓ | ✓ |
| Manage extensions | | ✗ | ✗ | ✗ | ✗ | ✗ | ✗ | ✓ | ✓ |
| Manage templates | | ✗ | ✗ | ✗ | ✗ | ✗ | ✗ | ✗ | ✓ |
| Manage site settings | | ✗ | ✗ | ✗ | ✗ | ✗ | ✗ | ✗ | ✓ |

You can see that each of these user groups build on each other. Each one has slightly more permissions than the last.

You can also see that only three of these user groups are allowed to access the administrator area: Manager, Administrator, and Super User. These three groups are particularly useful. You've seen the Super User group throughout this book. Let's see how different the Manager and Administrator groups are. Let's log in as those two groups. Here's how we do it:

- Go to "Users", "Manage", then "Add New User".

- I'm going to use "manager" for almost all of the entries, as shown in the image below:

| Account Details | Assigned User Groups | Basic Settings |
|---|---|---|
| Name * | manager | |
| Login Name * | manager | |
| Password | ••••••• | |
| Confirm Password | ••••••• | |
| Email * | manager@ostraining.com | |

- Click the "Assigned User Groups" tab.
- Check the "Manager" box. You don't have to uncheck the Registered box. This is because the Manager automatically gets all of the Registered user permissions, so checking or unchecking this box is unnecessary.

| Account Details | Assigned User Groups | Basic Settings |

☐ Public

☐ – Guest

☑ – Manager

☐ – Administrator

☑ – Registered

☐ – Author

☐ – Editor

☐ – Publisher

☐ – Super Users

- Click "Save & Close" and then use the "Logout" in the top-right corner.

- Go back to the administrator area and log in using the new Manager account.

You see a screen like the one below. Many of the drop-down menu options are gone. The Manager group has the ability to add and organize content. They can also use some of the components. However, they have very little ability to modify the site. They can't change the site's layout because they don't have access to the templates, modules, or menus. They also can't change any key settings because they don't have access to the Site Configuration screen or the Users link in the main drop-down menu.

Do you have any people updating your site who always make mistakes? Are you that person who always makes mistakes? If so, the Manager group is a great place to put them. They can add content safe in the knowledge that they really can't make any serious errors.

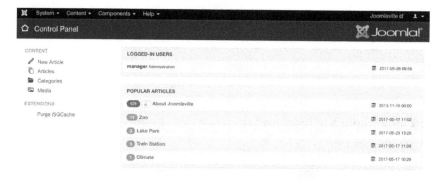

Now let's see what the Administrator group is like:

- Click "Logout" again and log in to the administrator area using the main Super User account that you've been using through the book.
- Go to "Users", "Manage".
- Click on the "Manager" user.

- Click the "Assigned User Groups" tab and check the Administrator box. You are now giving the Manager a promotion to the Administrator level.

- Click "Save & Close" and then "Logout" in the top-right corner.

- Log in again to the administrator area using the Manager account.

You now see a screen like the one below. The Administrator can do almost everything that the Super User can do.

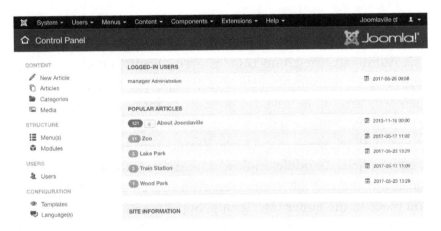

There is only one feature that the Administrator doesn't have access to. Go to "Users", then "Manage", and you see the users on the site.

Your Super User account has the ability to control the Registered, Manager and Administrator users? The opposite is not true. You won't be able to click on the Super User account. That's because the Administrator user can't edit the Super User, can't control them and can't demote them to a lower group. They also can't create a Super User.

| | Name ▲ | Username | Enabled | Activated | **User Groups** |
|---|---|---|---|---|---|
| ☐ | manager <br> 🗒 Add a Note <br> Advanced Permissions <br> Report | manager | ✓ | ✓ | Multiple groups |
| ☐ | registereduser <br> 🗒 Add a Note <br> Advanced Permissions <br> Report | registeredus er | ✓ | ✓ | Registered |
| | Steve Burge <br> 🗒 Add a Note <br> Advanced Permissions <br> Report | steve | Yes | ✓ | Super Users |

The Administrator group is great if you want to maintain final control over the site but give access to people who really know their way around Joomla. It's possible to make a lot of mistakes at the Administrator level, so be careful who you place in this group. For example, an Administrator can easily change the template, delete modules, upload extensions, and generally make a mess of the site. Of course, be even more careful about who you place in the Super User group. Super Users can do anything and everything on your site. So, for security reasons, I highly recommend that you put only a very small number of people in this group and place everyone else in the lower groups.

METHOD 3: CREATING YOUR OWN ACCESS CONTROLS

In Method 1, you saw five access levels: Guest, Public, Registered, Special and Super User.

In Method 2, you saw eight user groups: Public, Registered, Author, Editor, Publisher, Manager, Administrator, and Super Users.

In Method 3, you see how to change everything about those

access levels and user groups. You also see how you can create your own versions of them.

Let's give you an idea of how you can set up your own access controls. The example we use is someone whose only task is to add information about Joomlaville parks, but nothing else. Here's how we do it.

First we need to create the user group called Park Writer:

- Log in to your administrator area with your Super User account.
- Go "Users", "Groups", then "Add New Group".
- Group Title: **Park Writer**
- Group Parent: This choice is harder. My advice would be to choose the group that is closest to the one you want to create. You may want to review the Joomla User Chart and see what permissions you want to give to this group. In our example, Author is a good choice. We just want people in the Park Writer group to log in, write content, and edit their own content. No other permissions are necessary. If we choose Author, this new group automatically gets the Author's permissions.

## User Group Details

| Group Title * | Park Writer |
| --- | --- |
| Group Parent * | - - Author |

- Once you save your new group, you can see it listed in the tree, underneath the Author:

| | Group Title |
|---|---|
| ☐ | **Public**<br>Advanced Permissions Report |
| ☐ | – Guest<br>Advanced Permissions Report |
| ☐ | – Manager<br>Advanced Permissions Report |
| ☐ | – Administrator<br>Advanced Permissions Report |
| ☐ | – Registered<br>Advanced Permissions Report |
| ☐ | – Author<br>Advanced Permissions Report |
| ☐ | – Editor<br>Advanced Permissions Report |
| ☐ | – Publisher<br>Advanced Permissions Report |
| ☐ | – Park Writer<br>Advanced Permissions Report |
| ☐ | – Super Users<br>Advanced Permissions Report |

Second, we need to decide exactly what people in the Park Writer group can and cannot do. Each area of the site has its own permissions, so we need to go to the area that we're focusing on. In this example, we focus on controlling which categories the users can write in, so we need to go to the Category screen.

- Go to "Content", then "Categories".

Here's what we need to do: We need to stop people in the Park Writer group from creating content in all the categories except Parks. Because we based the Park Writer on the Author group, they currently have permission to create content in every category. We need to disable the content creation permission for the ParkWriter in all the categories except News. Let's see how that's done:

- Click on the "Uncategorised" category.
- Click on the "Permissions" tab.
- Click on "Park Writer":

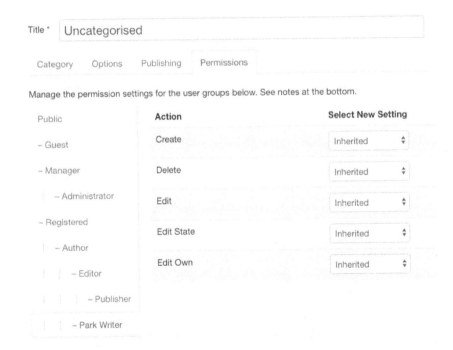

| Title * | Uncategorised | | |
|---|---|---|---|

Category    Options    Publishing    Permissions

Manage the permission settings for the user groups below. See notes at the bottom.

| Public | Action | Select New Setting |
|---|---|---|
| – Guest | Create | Inherited |
| – Manager | Delete | Inherited |
| – Administrator | Edit | Inherited |
| – Registered | Edit State | Inherited |
| – Author | Edit Own | Inherited |
| – Editor | | |
| – Publisher | | |
| – Park Writer | | |

You can see five available permissions:

- **Create:** The users can create new articles in this category.
- **Delete:** The users can delete articles in this category.

- **Edit:** The users can edit any articles in this category.

- **Edit State:** The users can publish and unpublish articles in this category.

- **Edit Own:** The users can edit their own articles in this category.

Currently, Park Writers can create and edit their own articles in this category.

We want to disable the News Writers ability to create and edit articles, so here's what we do:

- Change the "Create" setting to "Denied".

- Change the "Edit Own" setting to "Denied".

- Click "Save & Close".

- Repeat the process for the other categories, except for the Parks category.

This third step is the easiest. We just need to set up the user account and place them in the Park Writer group.

- Go to the "Users", "Manage", then "Add New User".

- Set up a new user. Give them a Name, Login Name, and Password. I'm going to use "parkwriter" for all of the settings except email.

- Click "Assigned User Groups" and click the "Park Writer" box.
- Click "Save & Close". Your screen should look like the one below.

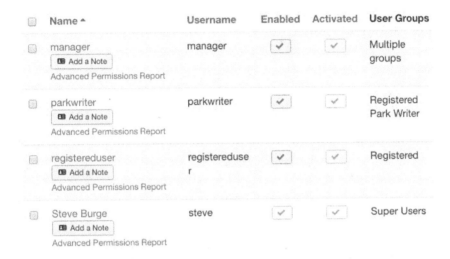

| | Name ▲ | Username | Enabled | Activated | **User Groups** |
|---|---|---|---|---|---|
| ☐ | manager<br>📇 Add a Note<br>Advanced Permissions Report | manager | ✔ | ✔ | Multiple groups |
| ☐ | parkwriter<br>📇 Add a Note<br>Advanced Permissions Report | parkwriter | ✔ | ✔ | Registered Park Writer |
| ☐ | registereduser<br>📇 Add a Note<br>Advanced Permissions Report | registereduse r | ✔ | ✔ | Registered |
| ☐ | Steve Burge<br>📇 Add a Note<br>Advanced Permissions Report | steve | ✔ | ✔ | Super Users |

The final step in this process is to check that we set everything up correctly:

- Go to the visitor area of your site and log in as the Park Writer.
- Click 'Submit an Article" in the User Menu module.

# Latest Articles

📄 Lake Park
📄 City Park
📄 Wood Park
📄 Train Station
📄 Bus Station

# User Menu

Your Profile

Submit an Article

- You'll see the article creation screen.
- Click the "Publishing" tab.
- The only category that the Park Writer can submit articles to is the Parks category:

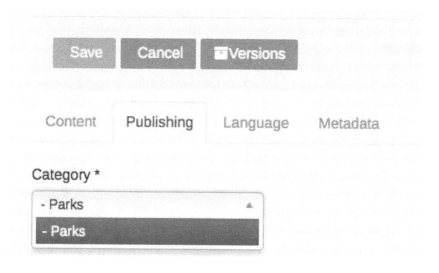

So that's the process for setting up a new user group on your site. To recap, here is the workflow we used:

- Step 1: Create a User Group
- Step 2: Decide the Permissions
- Step 3: Create the Users
- Step 4: Test

## WHAT'S NEXT?

Congratulations! You've now been through three methods for controlling Joomla users. Each method is more flexible but also more complex than the one before. Particularly with Method 3, things can become really powerful but also complicated. In this chapter, we only scratched the surface of what Method 3 could achieve on large sites. However, my advice is the same as at the beginning of the chapter: keep it simple. Managing five user levels or eight user groups is not too hard. Managing twenty five user levels or thirty eight user groups could become very complex. Keep on the side of simplicity.

In the final chapter of this book, we're going to show you how to keep your site safe and up-to-date.

Site Maintenance will be the final step in our Joomla workflow, as shown below. Remember that our first step was planning, and that took place before we even started building the site. Our last step takes place after we have finished building the site. Think of your website like a car or bicycle: once you start using it, inevitably it will need regular maintenance.

# CHAPTER 15.

# JOOMLA SITE MANAGEMENT EXPLAINED

---

Are you going to be responsible for maintaining your Joomla site? If so, this chapter is for you. This chapter shows you how to keep your site safe, secure, and updated.

Many of you will have other people to take care of these tasks for you. You might have a web design company, colleagues in the IT department, or other experienced people to help you out. If that's you, then you can happily skip this chapter.

However, if you are the person responsible for your site, then you need to know how to keep your site safe and secure. Among other things, you need to know how to protect your site and update it to the latest version.

After this chapter you'll be able to do the following:

- Update your site
- Update your extensions
- Disable or uninstall extensions
- Use additional measures to protect your site
- Back up your site
- Understand the Global Configuration screen

## UPDATING YOUR SITE

Treat your Joomla site as you treat your car.

All cars need regular maintenance and so do all Joomla sites. With a car, you need to pump up the tires, change the oil, change the battery, or do other fixes. With a Joomla site, you also need to apply fixes. Fortunately the most important of these fixes can be applied automatically using Joomla's update system.

Before we show you how to use Joomla's update system, you need to understand what you're updating to. Joomla's updates are based on version numbers, as described in the following section.

### An Overview of Joomla Version Numbers

Back in the chapter, "Joomla Explained", we talked a little about Joomla's version numbers. Some of the key points we mentioned are:

- You may encounter three major versions of Joomla:

  - Joomla 1 was released in 2008.

  - Joomla 2 was released in 2011.

  - Joomla 3 was released in 2012 and is the version we've used in this book.

- More versions will be released. Eventually there will be a Joomla 4 and even a Joomla 5.

- Different versions don't mean huge changes. New versions of Joomla are like new models of cars. This year's Toyota, Ford, or Honda might have small improvements or tweaks over last year's model, but it's instantly recognizable as the same car, and you'll have little problem moving from one to the other. Now that you've almost finished this book, you should be able to pick up a site using 1, 2, 3, or even a future version and be able to successfully use it.

Now let's get a little more specific about version numbers. Essentially they are two types: major versions and minor versions.

## Major versions

Major versions have large intervals between releases and often add important new features to Joomla.

- **Numbering:** Joomla 1, 2 and 3 are all major versions.
- **Reason for new major versions:** To add new features.
- **Importance:** Is it important to use the latest major version? It's useful but not essential. Because new major versions are released to add new features, there are no security problems if you don't upgrade. However, each major version is only supported by the Joomla team for so long, so yes, it's generally best to use the latest major version if possible.
- **Release dates:** Previously these versions were released whenever they were ready, but now the Joomla team has committed to releasing them every six months.
- **Updating:** It can sometimes be tricky to update, but the Joomla team has promised to make updates as easy as possible in the future, starting with the move from 3 to 4.

## Minor Versions

Minor versions are released irregularly but often and provide small fixes to existing features.

- **Numbering:** Each major version has minor versions, such as 3.5, 3.6, 3.7 and so on. There are even smaller versions such as 3.6.1, 3.6.2 and 3.6.3.
- **Reason for new minor versions:** Sometimes to add small features but mainly to fix security problems and bugs.
- **Importance:** Is it important to use the latest minor version?

Yes, absolutely. Because new minor versions are often released to fix security problems, it is vital to make sure you're using the latest version.

- **Release dates:** These versions are released approximately every one to two months, or as needed.
- **Updating:** In Joomla 3 you can update directly from your site's administrator area.

### What Version Do I Have?

Now that we understand what the numbers mean, let's see how to apply updates.

Go to the administrator area of your site and look at the bottom-right corner of the screen. You can see what version number you currently have. In the image below, the site is at version 3.7.2:

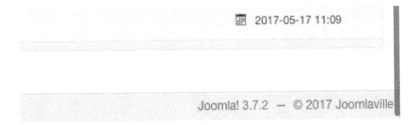

### How Do I Get Notified About Updates?

The best place to get update news is by logging into your site. If there is a new version of Joomla available, there will be clear messages. This message will be shown at the very top of your Joomla administrator area:

If you are the site administrator, you'll also receive an email which looks like this:

This email IS NOT sent by Joomla.org. It is sent automatically by your own site, OSTraining - https://www.ostraining.com/

===============================================================
UPDATE INFORMATION
===============================================================

Your site has discovered that there is an updated version of Joomla! available for download.

Joomla! version currently installed: 3.7.1
Joomla! version available for installation: 3.7.2

This email is sent to you by your site to remind you of this fact.
The Joomla! project will never contact you directly about available updates of Joomla! on your site.

===============================================================
UPDATE INSTRUCTIONS
===============================================================

To install the update on OSTraining please click the following link. (If the URL is not a link, simply copy & paste it to your browser).

## How Do I Update?

You can update Joomla with just a couple of clicks inside your site's administrator area. Here's how you do it:

- Go to "Components", then "Joomla Update!".

You'll see information about the available update, as shown in the image below:

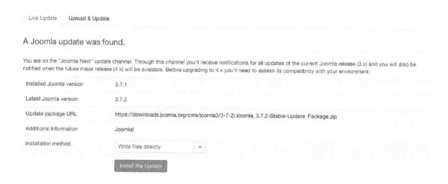

- Click "Install the Update" button.
- Joomla will show you a progress bar as your site updates:

Updating your Joomla files. Please wait ...

Percent complete 86.0
Bytes read 19744646
Bytes extracted 29568478
Files extracted

- You'll now see a success message:

## Joomla Version Update Status

Your site has been successfully updated. Your Joomla version is now 3.7.2.

## UPDATING YOUR EXTENSIONS

Just like every piece of software, Joomla is constantly evolving and changing. It's constantly being updated and improved. The same is true for your site's extensions. So, to keep your site safe, you may need to update your extensions as well as the main Joomla version. Components, modules, plugins and even language files need regular updates. Templates may occasionally need them, but they are likely to be much less frequent.

If your site has extensions that need updates, it will show them when you log into your site, as shown in the image below:

- Click the button "View Updates".
- You'll see a list of updates, as shown below:

| | Name ^ | Location | Type | Installed | Available | Folder | Install Type | URL Details |
|---|---|---|---|---|---|---|---|---|
| | OSMeta | Administrator | Component | 1.2.6 | 1.4.5 | N/A | Update | https://deploy.ostraining.com/client/update/pro/stable/com_osmeta https://github.com/OSTraining/OSMeta-Pro/releases/tag/v1.4.5 |
| | OSMyLicensesManager | Site | Plugin | 1.1.4 | 1.2.5 | system | Update | https://deploy.ostraining.com/client/update/free/stable/plg_system_osmylicensesmanager https://github.com/OSTraining/OSMyLicensesManager/releases/tag/v1.2.5 |

- Click the check boxes for all the updates.
- Click the "Update" button in the top-left corner.
- You'll now see a success message, as shown below:

**Message**

System plugin ossystem was successfully updated
Osmap plugin joomla was successfully updated
Updating component was successful.

**OSMap - the easiest way to create a Joomla sitemap.**

# Thanks for updating OSMap!

It's worth noting that this method of updating works for almost all, but not all extensions. Some old extensions don't allow updates via this method, so the best thing to do is check the documentation available for the extension. Here are two common ways for older extensions to update:

- Some extensions can be updated by downloading the new version and installing it manually. The extension automatically recognizes and overwrites the older version, leaving all your data intact.

- Some extensions have their own automatic update tool inside their own their component area in your administrator.

## DISABLING OR UNINSTALLING YOUR EXTENSIONS

For security reasons, it's important to delete any extensions that you're not using. If extensions are unused, you're also more likely to forget about updating them. Older extensions that haven't been regularly updated are more likely to suffer from security holes. Here's how you can remove those unused extensions:

- Go to "Extensions", "Manage", then "Manage".

- Search or scroll down to find the extension you want to delete. In this example, I searched for OSMap. Check the box next to all parts of the extension. For example, in the image below you can see that OSMap has both the plugin and component.

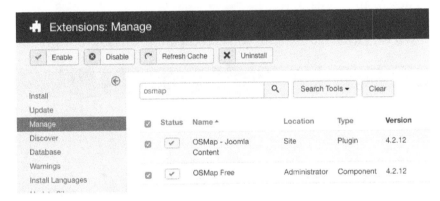

- Click the "Uninstall" button.
- You'll see a message that the uninstall was successful:

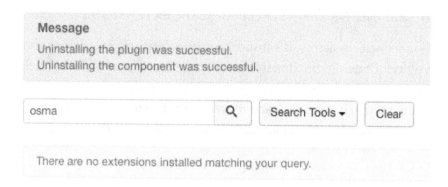

The Extension Manager also allows you to disable an extension without deleting it. Why would you want to do this? Perhaps the most common reasons are because your administrator area is becoming cluttered, but you aren't completely sure if you want to delete an extension.

- On the "Manage" screen, you can click the "Disable button":

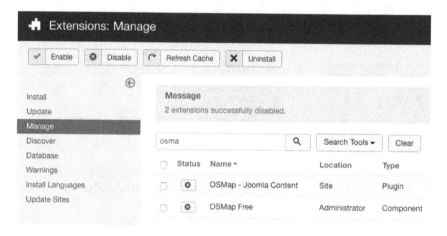

## ADDITIONAL MEASURES TO PROTECT YOUR SITE

There are some extensions available that add extra security features to your site. One of the best is called Admin Tools. Here's how to use it:

- Go to "Extensions", then "Install" and search for "Admin

Tools". In the category tree, it is under "Access & Security", then "Site Security". The Admin Tools page is shown below:

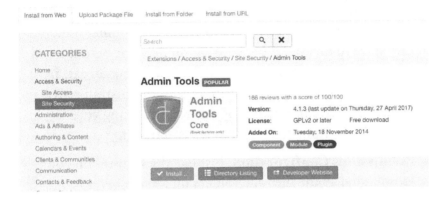

- Click "Install" and then click "Install" again.

- You'll see a message confirming that Admin Tools was successfully installed.

- Go to "Components", then "Admin Tools". You see a screen like the one below:

Here are three of the important security features provided by Admin Tools.

- **Password-Protect Administrator:** By default, anyone can access the administrator login form for any Joomla site. All they have to do is add the word /administrator onto the end of the site's URL. This feature allows you to put an extra username and password in front of the administrator area and greatly decrease the chance of someone guessing your login, or using an automated script to try and find it.

- **Permissions Configuration:** Just like the features on your Joomla site, all the files and folders on a Web server have permissions that decide who is allowed to access and use them. To take a simple example, your /images/ directory allows Joomla users to upload and view images, but general visitors can only view the images. If you understand how file and folder permissions work, you can modify them from here.

- **Fix Permissions:** If you don't understand how file and folder permissions work, this feature can set them to a safe setting automatically.

Admin Tools also has a Professional version with dozens more security features. The 20 Euros it costs to upgrade to the Professional version is well worth the cost, and it's an important part of how we protect our sites.

## BACKING UP YOUR SITE

It's important to keep your site secure, but even the best sites can run into problems, and even the best site administrators can make mistakes. To recover from serious problems and errors, you need to have backups. There are two main ways to make backups: Your hosting company can do it, and you can do it yourself. I recommend that you set up both options.

## Backups Made by Your Hosting Company

Many of the best hosting companies make backups for their clients. Some of the best hosts will not only make the backups but also give you the ability to restore a backup in place of the current site.

Some other hosts make the backups but require that you contact them and ask for the backup to be restored.

Finally, some hosts won't make any backups at all available to you as they create backups to recover from server failure and not your mistakes.

It's important that you know the backup policy of your host, whether it's good, mediocre, or bad.

## Backups Made by You

The same developer who created the Admin Tools extension also created a useful extension for backing up and restoring your Joomla site. The name of the extension is Akeeba Backup. We show you how to use it so that you can back up sites by yourself. Here's how to use Akeeba Backup:

- Go to "Extensions", then "Install" and search for "Akeeba Backup". In the category tree, it is under Access & Security, then Site Security, and then Backup. The Akeeba Backup page is shown below:

- Click "Install" and then click "Install" again.

- Go to "Components", then "Akeeba Backup". You see a pop-up window offering to configure the extension for you. Click the green "Configuration Wizard" button, as seen below:

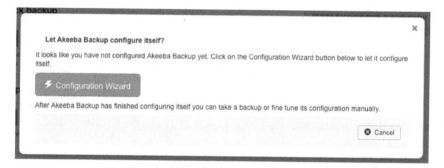

- Akeeba Backup will now configure itself to work correctly on your site. You'll see it analyzing your site:

- When the process has finished, you'll see a message saying Finished Benchmarking. Click on the blue "Backup Now" button:

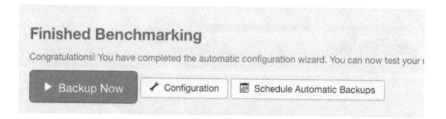

- You're now ready to start a backup. Click on the blue "Backup Now" button:

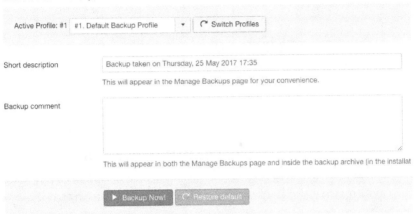

- During the backup process, Akeeba Backup shows another progress bar like the one below and tells you what it's working on:

- When the process is over, you see a message saying "Backup Completed Successfully". Click on the "Manage Backups" button to go and download your backup:

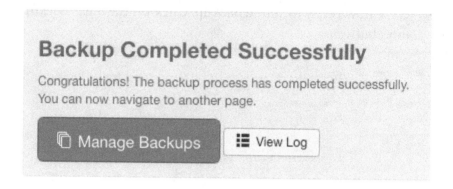

**Backup Completed Successfully**

Congratulations! The backup process has completed successfully. You can now navigate to another page.

📋 Manage Backups    ☰ View Log

- You now see a list of your backups. Look under the Manage & Download column and click on the green "Download" button. That downloads the backup files to your desktop. From there you can store the backups in a safe place on your hard drive or elsewhere.

Remember that all hosting is different, and you might run into problems while creating backups. If you do, the Akeeba Backup website at http://akeebabackup.com is an excellent source of information. It has further documentation on how you can use the extension in more advanced ways. For example, you can create backups automatically and send the backups to remote storage provided by companies such as Amazon and Dropbox.

The Akeeba Backup site also provides a file called Akeeba Kickstart, which allows you to extract and restore the backup that you made.

The extension is thoroughly documented and is well worth

exploring further if you want to make sure that your site has safe and regular backups.

## GLOBAL CONFIGURATION

There is one final, important part of the Joomla administrator area that we haven't covered: Global Configuration. We have been into this area occasionally during this book, but now is the time to explore it in detail. Go ahead and click on Global Configuration under Site in the main drop-down menu, and you see a screen like the one below. There are many options in here, so I won't take you through them all but explain those that are the most useful and important.

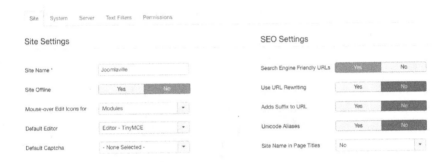

### Taking Your Site Offline

One of the most useful options available inside Global Configuration is the ability to take your site offline. You can use this setting while you're getting a site ready for launch, or if you want to take it offline while making improvements. Here's how you use it:

- In Global Configuration, check the box setting "Site Offline" to "Yes". You can use the "Offline Message" and "Custom Message" boxes to write a note to show visitors:

- Click "Save & Close". Go to the visitor area of your site, and your site looks like the image below. People who don't have a username and password at a sufficiently high level won't be able to log in.

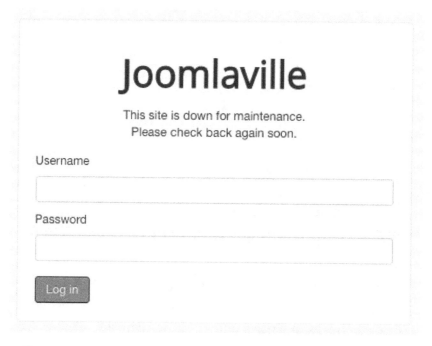

- Enter your username and password that you normally use to get into the administrator area of your site. You now can see, edit, and browse around your site without any restrictions.

- As soon as you're ready to make your site live again, go to the administrator area and Global Configuration, set "Site Offline" to "No", and click "Save & Close".

- If you want to change the logo that people see when the site is offline, go to the Global Configuration. You can upload your site's logo for the offline page by using the "Offline Image" setting.

## Metadata Settings

To be honest, I'm including these options to try and clear up the confusion around them, rather than because they are useful. We get a lot of questions about them from our students in class. We normally tell them not to touch the settings at all and just leave the default choices in place. The settings are shown in the image below, and here's a rundown of what they do:

- **Site Meta Description:** This text may appear under your site title in search engine results. However, to be worthwhile, each description needs to be unique for the page it's on. Therefore, I recommend leaving this field blank because no single description can correctly apply to all the pages on your site. Instead, make sure to fill in the Meta Description inside each article. Even if you don't, search engines read the text on your site and create a description.

- **Site Meta Keywords:** Search engines almost entirely ignore keywords included in your metadata because so many people tried to misuse that feature for spam. It's much more important to have keywords in your main article text instead.

- **Content Rights:** This tag shows information about who holds the copyright for the content on the site. Often copyright information is complex enough that the best thing to do is include a link in here to a full page of copyright information.

- **Show Author Meta Tag:** This setting can be left as Yes. It shows the author of the content, as listed in the article, inside the metadata.

- **Show Joomla Version:** This setting can also be left as No. This would show your Joomla version number inside the metadata.

## Metadata Settings

| | |
|---|---|
| Site Meta Description | A great place to learn Joomla |
| Site Meta Keywords | |
| Robots | Index, Follow ▾ |
| Content Rights | |
| Show Author Meta Tag | Yes \| No |
| Show Joomla Version | Yes \| No |

### Changing Your Site's URLs

So, we dismissed the Metadata Settings as having little impact on your site's search engine rankings. However, these next settings will likely have a greater impact and will also make your site more usable for visitors. We explain how to change Joomla's URLs.

I have two warnings before we begin:

- These settings are more responsible for more people saying "Help, my site has crashed!" than anything else in the history of Joomla. Fortunately the fix is simple: If you change any of these settings to Yes and your site starts producing broken links, simply change the settings back to No again. At the end of this section we have some suggestions for making these settings work if they cause problems on your site.

- It is best to get these settings right before you launch your site. If you change them later, they can cause broken links and frustration for your visitors.

To change your URLs, look inside your Global Configuration for the SEO Settings, as shown in the image below:

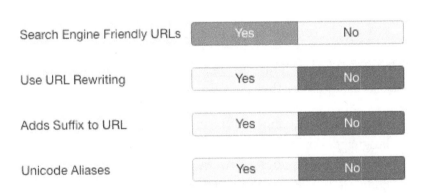

These four settings modify the URLs on your site. The difference between choosing "Yes" or "No" can be major. Here are two examples for the same article. The choices are cumulative, so you must turn on "Search Engine Friendly URLs" before turning on "Add Suffix to URL".

- **Search Engine Friendly URLs:** This setting radically shortens and improves the URLs.

- **Yes:** http://ostraining.com/index.php/category-name/article-name
- **No:** http://ostraining.com/index.php?option=com_content&view=article-name&id=1:joomla&catid=2:category-name&Itemid=101

- **Use URL rewriting:** This setting removes /index.php/ from the URLs.

  - **Yes:** http://ostraining.com/category-name/article-name
  - **No:** http://ostraining.com/index.php/2-category-name/1-article-name

- **Adds Suffix to URL:** This setting adds .html to the end of the URLs.

  - **Yes:** http://ostraining.com/category-name/article-name.html
  - **No:** http://ostraining.com/category-name/article-name

- **Unicode Aliases:** This setting is only for people running their site in a language other than English.

  - **Yes:** Your URLs show in the characters of the native language. For example, Greek Web sites will have URLs using Greek characters, Arabic Web sites will use Arabic characters, Chinese Web sites will use Chinese characters, and so on.
  - **No:** Your URLs will be show in A-to-Z characters only.

Here are my recommendations for those settings:

- **Search Engine Friendly URLs:** Yes. This setting radically shortens and improves the URLs.
- **Use URL rewriting:** Yes. This makes the URLs shorter and /index.php/ doesn't add anything useful to the URLs.

- **Adds Suffix to URL:** No. We're not building HTML Web sites any longer, and it doesn't make much sense to extend the URLs with .html.

- **Unicode Aliases:** No, if you're running your site in English or any language that primarily uses A-Z and 0-9 characters. If you're using a language with another character set, choose Yes if you think your users will prefer to use those characters rather than A-Z and 0-9.

- **Include Site Name in Page Titles:** Yes. It's important to show people what the name of your site is. However, make sure that your site name is short, accurate, and helps people identify your site.

So, if these settings can produce much better URLs, why are they not all turned on by default? It's because not all hosting companies work well with these settings, and Joomla's default settings are those that work on the largest number of servers. If your server has problems with these settings, you'll see blank pages and broken URLs on your site until they are turned off. So what can you do if you see these problems?

- **Turn off some settings:** As mentioned, the first three SEO settings are cumulative. For example, "Use URL rewriting" has more complex requirements to work than does "Search Engine Friendly URLs". So, try turning off some of the settings.

- **Rename the htaccess.txt file to .htaccess:** This is a useful feature for your URLs but also for your site's security.

Here's how you can rename your .htaccess file:

- Back in the chapter, "Joomla Installations Explained". we showed how to use FTP software, such as Filezilla to upload Joomla to a web server. We need that same software for this task. Log in to your server where Joomla is hosted.

- In the main directory of your Joomla files, look for a file called htaccess.txt.

- Rename the file to .htaccess. If there is already a file called .htaccess, you need to rename that other file first.

### Making Your Site Run Faster

There are two settings inside Global Configuration that make your site run faster and reduce the amount of work your site needs to do.

First, and simplest, is Gzip Page Compression. All those extensions and templates that you downloaded have used the same Gzip compression. It compresses all the files into smaller versions, without damaging them, so that they move around the web more quickly. If your whole site is compressed, that means that visitors get a compressed version of your site that reaches them more quickly and therefore takes less time to load.

- To change the setting, click on the "Server" tab and look for "Gzip Page Compression" inside the "Server" tab. Change the setting to "Yes":

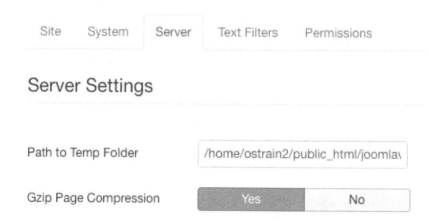

Second, and a little more involved, is Cache. Whereas Gzip Page Compression makes your site much smaller, the Cache setting freezes it. What does that mean? Every time a visitor arrives at your site, Joomla needs to do a lot of work. It needs to check which template is being used, which modules are needed, which articles or components should appear on the page, and also check a lot of things to make sure the page displays correctly for the visitor. All those checks take time, and Joomla repeats the process for each new visitor. Cache solves that problem by freezing the page and delivering the same version to each visitor. Joomla doesn't have to re-create the page each time, and so everything loads much more quickly.

The downside to Cache is that the information may become out-of-date if it freezes for too long. Joomla solves that problem by deleting the Cache after a fixed period of time and then creating a new, frozen version.

- Turn the Cache on by clicking on the "System tab inside "Global Configuration" and changing the "System Cache" setting to "ON – Progressive caching". You can see the setting in the image below:

## Cache Settings

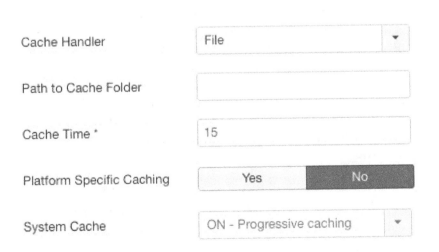

| | |
|---|---|
| Cache Handler | File |
| Path to Cache Folder | |
| Cache Time * | 15 |
| Platform Specific Caching | Yes / No |
| System Cache | ON - Progressive caching |

Three more things to note about the Cache:

- It's not helpful if you're making a lot of edits on the site, because every time you make an edit, you'll still be looking at the version from 15 minutes ago.

- If you find problems with your site after turning on the cache, try turning this setting down to "ON – Conservative caching".

- You can reset the Cache at any time by going to "System", and clicking on "Clear Cache".

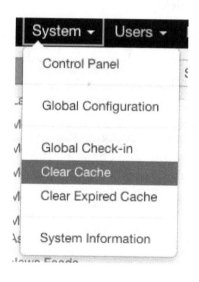

WHAT'S NEXT?

Congratulations! You've reached the end of Joomla 3 Explained.

So what's next?

- **Practice:** The only way to get better at Joomla is to build Joomla sites. Decide on your first Joomla project and start practicing.

- **Practice now:** You will forget most of what you've read in this book. That's human nature and doesn't make me a bad teacher or you a bad learner. The longer you wait to practice

Joomla, the more you'll forget. Why not get started right away?

- **Learn more:** I guarantee that there are things you will come across while using Joomla that haven't been included in this book. This book has only a limited number of pages, and we've tried to focus on only the most important things about Joomla. However, one of the great things about Joomla being so popular is that almost every problem you run into has been encountered by other people. Many of those people will have asked for or posted a solution to their problem online. If you ever get stuck, here are the first places you should go to for help:

  - http://ostraining.com. This is my company's site. We have thousands of Joomla tutorials and videos. My email address is steve@ostraining.com. Email me with questions!

  - http://google.com. If you get an error message or encounter a problem, type it directly into a search engine, and there's a good chance you'll find a solution.

  - http://forum.joomla.org. The Joomla forums have around 3 million posts at the time of writing, so there are a lot of solutions to be found. Search for a solution to your question, and if you don't find it, write a new post. There's sure to be someone able to help you.

- **Join the Joomla community.** Joomla doesn't rely on money; it relies on people like you. Whether you attend a local Joomla event, post solutions you find on the forum, or even say thank you to someone who's helped you, there are many easy ways to become part of the Joomla community. The more you rely on Joomla for your Web site or your business, the more it will benefit you to become part of the community.

I hope to see you around in the Joomla community, and I wish you all the best in your use of Joomla!